We Deserve Better Villains

We Deserve Better Villains

A Video Game Design Survival Guide

By Jai Kristjan

CRC Press
Taylor & Francis Group
Boca Raton London New York

CRC Press is an imprint of the
Taylor & Francis Group, an **informa** business

CRC Press
Taylor & Francis Group
6000 Broken Sound Parkway NW, Suite 300
Boca Raton, FL 33487-2742

Printed on acid-free paper

International Standard Book Number-13: 978-0-367-18479-7 (paperback)
978-0-367-18480-3 (hardback)

Library of Congress Cataloging-in-Publication Data

Names: Kristjan, Jai, author.
Title: We deserve better villains : a video game design survival guide / Jai Kristjan.
Description: Boca Raton, FL : Taylor & Francis, 2019.
Identifiers: LCCN 2019005976| ISBN 9780367184797 (pbk. : alk. paper) | ISBN 9780367184803 (hardback : alk. paper)
Subjects: LCSH: Video games—Design. | Video game characters—Design.
Classification: LCC GV1469.3 .K75 2019 | DDC 794.8—dc23
LC record available at https://lccn.loc.gov/2019005976

Visit the Taylor & Francis Web site at
http://www.taylorandfrancis.com

and the CRC Press Web site at
http://www.crcpress.com

Special Thanks

To my mother, Donna Kristjan, who raised me up, taught me right, and understood when I found that games made me happy.

To my lady love, Emily Megan, who gave me the space to write this book in the first place, loves me for being who I am, and never stops pushing me forward.

To my friends Milo Casali, Ben Jones, Mark McKevitt, Stuart Ure, Jesse Weymer, Brad Anderson, and Mike Kerr, who stand beside me, hold my head up when I need it, and are the best bunch of lads to spend an evening with. They keep me sane when the world is filled with insanity.

To my favorite manager, Edward Illing, who saw more in me than I did, supported me when all others would not, and taught me more about being a better person at work than anyone yet.

To my first mentor, Terry Coleman, who taught me to breathe, be patient, and be great at what I was doing. His lessons are the base of my temple.

And finally, to Lisa Voisin, whose experience, editing ability and knowledge of the publishing world helped make this book possible. I am eternally grateful.

Contents

Preface, xiii

Chapter 1 ▪ Preparation 1

THE GAME BEGINS: PREPARATION 2
PREPARATION DEFINITION 4
PREPARATION: THE QUEST 6
PREPARATION: YOUR CREW 7
PREPARATION: YOUR ENVIRONMENT 8

Chapter 2 ▪ Blue Sky 11

LEVEL 2: BLUE SKY 12
BLUE SKY DEFINITION 14
BLUE SKY: CORE IDEA 16
BLUE SKY: RESEARCH 17
BLUE SKY: SHOOT FOR THE MOON 18
BLUE SKY: IDEAS ARE YOURS OR THEIRS 19
BLUE SKY: BREAK IT DOWN, BREAK IT DOWN, BREAK IT DOWN 21
BLUE SKY: THEORY VS. PRACTICAL 22
BLUE SKY: VISION 24
BLUE SKY: DON'T BE AT HOME FOR FEAR 25
BLUE SKY: CHOOSE A COLOR SCHEME 27
BLUE SKY: POSSIBILITIES AND SOLUTIONS 28
BLUE SKY: REPLAY-ABILITY 29

BLUE SKY: TO STORY OR NOT TO STORY 31
BLUE SKY: TARGET AUDIENCE 32
BLUE SKY: DESIGN IS NOT JUST IN GAMES—LOOK OUTSIDE 33

CHAPTER 3 ▪ Pre-production 35

LEVEL 3: PRE-PRODUCTION 36
PRE-PRODUCTION DEFINITION 38
PRE-PRODUCTION: DURATION 40
PRE-PRODUCTION: DESIGN DOCUMENT 41
PRE-PRODUCTION: GRAND DESIGN DOCUMENT VS. MICRO DESIGN DOCS 42
PRE-PRODUCTION: WRITE FOR YOUR AUDIENCE 44
PRE-PRODUCTION: PROTOTYPE OR SUFFER 45
PRE-PRODUCTION: BACKSTORY 46
PRE-PRODUCTION: EVOKING EMOTIONS 48
PRE-PRODUCTION: THREE LEVELS OF COMPLEXITY 49
PRE-PRODUCTION: INNOVATION VS. BOILERPLATE 50
PRE-PRODUCTION: MAKE A MODEL 52
PRE-PRODUCTION: MICRO ADVENTURES 53
PRE-PRODUCTION: LIGHTS, CAMERA, CAMERA 55
PRE-PRODUCTION: TOOLS—LOOK TO THE FUTURE 56
PRE-PRODUCTION: AUDIO DESIGN 57
PRE-PRODUCTION: MONETIZATION 59
PRE-PRODUCTION: PLATFORM OR PLATFORMS 60
PRE-PRODUCTION: COMMUNICATE EARLY 61
PRE-PRODUCTION: CHARACTER GROWTH 63
PRE-PRODUCTION: CONTROLS 64
PRE-PRODUCTION: DIVERSITY 65
PRE-PRODUCTION: LOCALIZATION 67
PRE-PRODUCTION: FALLING DOWN THE RABBIT HOLE 68

CHAPTER 4 ■ Production 71

LEVEL 4: PRODUCTION 72
PRODUCTION DEFINITION 74
PRODUCTION: EVALUATE EACH MILESTONE 76
PRODUCTION: CTRL-X 77
PRODUCTION: COMMUNICATION CATCH-UP 78
PRODUCTION: MAINTAINING THE BALANCE 80
PRODUCTION: YOUR TIME IS PRECIOUS 81
PRODUCTION: MAKE VILLAINS VIBRANT 82
PRODUCTION: BUILD PARTS TO COMBINE 84
PRODUCTION: TEST YOUR STUFF 85
PRODUCTION: INCENTIVES 86
PRODUCTION: PEAKS AND VALLEYS 88
PRODUCTION: VISUAL STORYTELLING 89
PRODUCTION: YOU ARE NOT YOUR MISTAKES 90
PRODUCTION: SPIDERWEB OF FEATURES 92
PRODUCTION: RISK VS. REWARD 93
PRODUCTION: TUNE IT 94
PRODUCTION: DIFFICULTY 96
PRODUCTION: LEVEL DESIGN 97
PRODUCTION: WHAT ARE YOU DOING RIGHT NOW? 99
PRODUCTION: GOAL SETTING 100
PRODUCTION: ARTIFICIAL INTELLIGENCE 101
PRODUCTION: FINAL FEATURE 103
PRODUCTION: THE POWER IS NOT IN DESIGN 104
PRODUCTION: READY, STEADY, GO! 106
PRODUCTION: ALL HAIL CHAOS 107
PRODUCTION: KEEP IT STABLE 108
PRODUCTION: FRIENDS MAKE LIFE BETTER 110

CHAPTER 5 ▪ Alpha 113

LEVEL 5: ALPHA 114
ALPHA DEFINITION 116
ALPHA: BUGS 118
ALPHA: 125% 119
ALPHA: IMPORTANCE OF 100% FIX RATE 120
ALPHA: THE ART OF BUG BALANCE 122
ALPHA: TEST THE GAME! 123
ALPHA: ASK FOR HELP 125
ALPHA: MARATHONER VS. SPRINTER 126
ALPHA: HELP OTHERS 127
ALPHA: OVERTIME MADNESS 129
ALPHA: THE SACRED ART OF THE PIVOT 130
ALPHA: LOVE QA, DON'T HATE THEM 132
ALPHA: OH, IT'S NEW, WE SHOULD DO THAT 133
ALPHA: UPDATING DESIGN RATHER THAN GETTING THE GAME DONE 134
ALPHA: BUILD A FOLLOWING 136
ALPHA: DEMOS, AKA PURE EVIL 137
ALPHA: GET IT OUT EARLY 138
ALPHA: REMEMBER *YOU* IN ALL OF THIS 140

CHAPTER 6 ▪ Beta 143

LEVEL 6: BETA 144
BETA DEFINITION 146
BETA: JOHNNY OR JANIE ON THE SPOT 148
BETA: CHECK EVERY BUG YOURSELF 149
BETA: KNOW YOUR GAME 150
BETA: MONOTONY 152
BETA: PLAY YOUR GAME 153
BETA: PLAY WHERE THE PLAYER PLAYS 154
BETA: HERDING CATS 156

BETA: RELAX—IT'S IN EVERYONE'S BEST INTEREST 157
BETA: PREPARE YOURSELF FOR INTERVIEWS 159
BETA: LOVE QA EVEN MORE 160

CHAPTER 7 ▪ Final 163

LEVEL 7: FINAL 164
FINAL DEFINITION 166
FINAL: CHART YOUR SHIPPED BUGS 168
FINAL: GIVE UP ON PRAISE 169
FINAL: DUST OFF YOUR BLUE SKY NOTES 170
FINAL: DO A POSTMORTEM 172
FINAL: CELEBRATE YOUR VICTORIES 173

CHAPTER 8 ▪ Post-release 175

LEVEL 8: POST-RELEASE 176
POST-RELEASE DEFINITION 178
POST-RELEASE: IT'S ALIVE, KILL IT NOW! 180
POST-RELEASE: PATCH PLAN—HAVE ONE 181
POST-RELEASE: VISIT YOUR PRODUCT IN THE STORES 182
POST-RELEASE: REVIEW SCORES AND BOTTOM LINE 184
POST-RELEASE: PUT IT ON THE WALL 185
POST-RELEASE: NOTHING TO DO IS A STATE OF MIND 186
POST-RELEASE: BE WORKING ON SOMETHING ALREADY 188
POST-RELEASE: WHAT HAPPENS WHEN YOU WIN 189

CHAPTER 9 ▪ Live 191

LEVEL 9: LIVE 192
LIVE DEFINITION 194
LIVE: YOU FIGHT FOR THE USERS 196
LIVE: LIVE WILL SCHOOL YOU 197

LIVE: FIX THE BOAT BEFORE MAKING A NEW ONE 198
LIVE: FROM TROLLS TO HEROES 200
LIVE: A/B/C/D … Q TESTING 201
LIVE: DLC FOR YOU AND ME 202
LIVE: WORKFLOW WAVES 204

CHAPTER 10 ▪ Miscellaneous 207

LEVEL 0: MISCELLANEOUS 208
MISCELLANEOUS OR EVERYTHING ELSE 210
MISCELLANEOUS: THE WRITTEN WORD 211
MISCELLANEOUS: THE POWERLESS UM 212
MISCELLANEOUS: PRESENTATION PREPARATION 214
MISCELLANEOUS: ART OF THE PRESENTATION 215
MISCELLANEOUS: STORYTELLING 216
MISCELLANEOUS: SILENT BUT DEADLY 217
MISCELLANEOUS: INTERFACE DESIGN 219
MISCELLANEOUS: SYSTEMS DESIGNERS 220
MISCELLANEOUS: CONTENT DESIGNERS 221
MISCELLANEOUS: LEVEL DESIGNERS 223
MISCELLANEOUS: AUDIO DESIGNERS 224
MISCELLANEOUS: SEE-MORES 225
MISCELLANEOUS: 30-DAY DESIGN CHALLENGE 227

CONCLUSION, 229

INDEX, 231

Preface

We deserve better villains. And not just villains—we deserve better everything in video games. Right now that isn't happening, and instead of looking outward to blame the world it's time to look to ourselves as video game designers. Over the last 15 years I have seen all manner of game designers, from self-taught to scholastically trained, yet every group is missing the practical understanding of what needs to be done when making a game in the development cycle. This practical or tribal knowledge is not being passed along which means that games are routinely starting again from scratch, destined to repeat the same mistakes. This can be seen across the entire industry of games, and players wonder why we don't make classics like we used to. Well, it's plainly because video game designers just don't have the experience to call on anymore. Instead of letting this happen any longer I want to take a stand, to plant my flag in the ground, raise my sword and yell, "NOT AGAIN, NOT EVER." This book is the direct result of me fighting for all games to be better—I can save a few every year, but it's time to help everyone. Your job is to learn and apply it 'cause, dammit, I WANT BETTER VILLAINS!

Now, after my blustering to get your attention, I want to be clear that this isn't some manifesto or revolutionary document. It's an easily digestible outline of periods of a video game project cycle with specifics on what a designer is supposed to be doing during each period to succeed. Each section explains what should be on the mind of a designer for that period coupled with helpful points to get the job done. It's always about action. To make sure this book gets read, enjoyed, and used I took a few things into consideration that you the reader need to understand.

One, each point is condensed down to make it easily understood. Read, digest, think, and act on it. This is a direct result of today's media, which has taught people to access information at a dazzling speed, which means we pick up knowledge in bite-sized intervals. You can blame television, the web, and your phone for this, all of which the general populace has devoured whole, demanding more every day. I think humans by nature have always wanted for information and that leads me to make it as easy to get into each point instead of wasting your time with chapters of useless exposition. I chose to keep it lean and clean to stick with you.

Two, it's a journey and like many great adventures it's about the experience, not the end result. You might think it's about seeing the game you have worked so hard on ready for purchase by players. It's not. While that is a step in the process, it's not the result which these pages will teach you. I explain this journey through video game tropes/situations at the beginning of each chapter to help you better understand the beginning, middle, and end using a fictitious video game as the setting to allow you to go through it in a narrative—everyone likes to be told a story. As a designer you are an active member of a team to drive a game's success but never think that you are the sole hero. "Hero" is another word for a person who gets other people killed. You want to be the survivor who will live to make more games rather than grabbing the accolades of just one and exiting stage left as the music comes up to drown out your speech.

Three, this is a survival guide and not about a specific genre of games. That means this is a high-level blanket statement style of book that details periods of games development, points to understand what is going on, and what actions you can take to make sure you are on the path to surviving the project, which applies to any genre. You don't become a designer to make just one style of game. You need to understand how to deal with the games development cycle across any game, as this book allies with all. Few people ever get it right the first time, which means you surviving equates to you growing and learning to make better games. This book is more or less a cheat sheet from my years of experience to help you survive. Plus, I have added a section to get you into action for each point and to remind you that design is about doing, not just thinking.

So why the hell did I write this? Well, let me tell you a story, as one of the best gifts of knowledge I learned is that the best designer in the room is the one who can tell the best story. So I'll begin. Many years ago on my first day as a junior game designer, I sat at my new desk, read the emails of the group I didn't understand, and by noon I was handed a book on game design by my design lead and told to read it front to back before I spoke to him again. Being new to the whole designer position, I did what I was told, and when I was done I realized that I had learned more than I expected from its pages. First off, I realized I didn't like reading one person's antiquated view on game design. Second, it focused on a product I had never heard of by a person halfway around the world in a genre I was not working on. And third, my lead had little to no time to teach me anything, as he needed a slave to repeat the words, "Yes, you're right" along with doing his design work for him. Luckily the gods of design had a different path for me—that project got shelved in two months, the lead took a job in another city, never to be heard from again, I was transferred to another department and amazingly dumped into the path of a wonderful designer who had one simple design philosophy: what are you doing right now to make the game better? That was a breath of fresh air and became my mantra across countless games and products. I have never stopped trying to make the games I worked on the best they could be. I told a friend that story in a pub one night, and he told me I should write a book to save others from what I had learned. Well, to be frank, he was drunk and told me to save the world of games, with great emotional gusto. After that night I realized I should do my best to help the world around me if I could influence even one person to improve. We would all do better as a people if we gave without need of reward.

Enjoy the read, experience all that you can, and be better than you are today for yourself as well as the games you create.

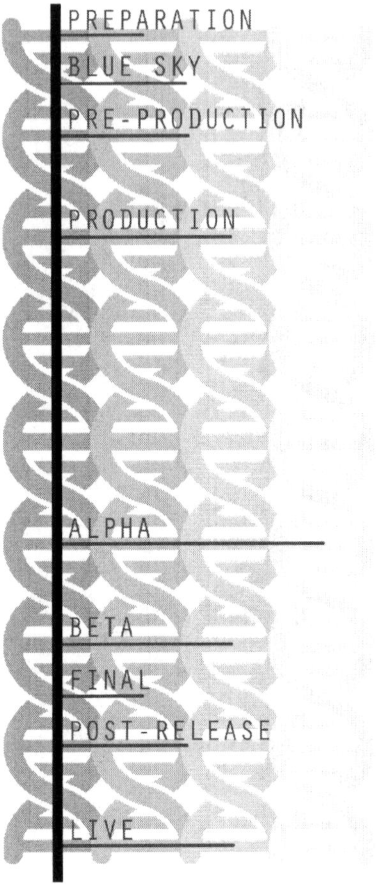

PREPARATION
BLUE SKY
PRE-PRODUCTION
PRODUCTION
ALPHA
BETA
FINAL
POST-RELEASE
LIVE

CHAPTER 1

Preparation

CONTENTS

The Game Begins: Preparation 2
Preparation Definition 4
Preparation: The Quest 6
Preparation: Your Crew 7
Preparation: Your Environment 8

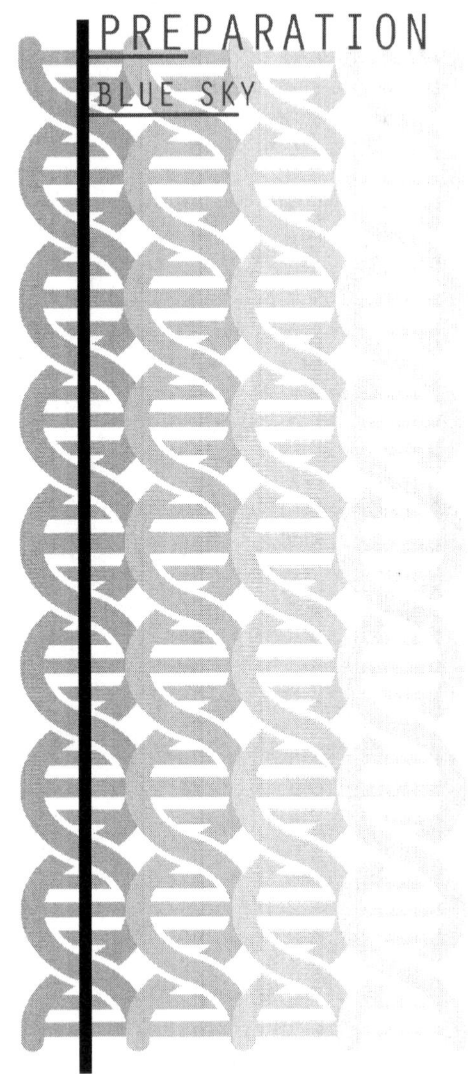

THE GAME BEGINS: PREPARATION

We start every adventure with excitement. We are called to action the moment we push the Play button. You're presented with the basics of the game, with your job boiled down to survival—get to the end and rewards will be yours. Sounds easy, right? Well, if you knew what it was really going to be like, you might just turn around, slam the Play button door in the player's face, and hang a sign on the door that politely told them to go have sex with themselves. We don't take up all calls to action, just like we don't play every game that comes out. We pick and choose what makes the most sense to us according to our own enjoyment. Once we decide to play, we act on it, and this is a powerful thing. Any old loser can just sit around.

Eventually, after some convincing through cutscenes, dialogue, and non-player characters pleading with you, you decide to take up the quest. You want this to be a valuable use of your time. You also need to put food on the table and keep a roof over your head. You do this by working for a games company, where you exchange your services for money through the vocation of video game design. You count yourself lucky to be in such a class of character, as you had to roll a few times before it came up as a default.

Now, before any adventure you need to take stock of your character. This means checking yourself mentally for the journey, understanding the system you're about to have to follow to get to the end, what allies will be joining you, and where this entire escapade will take place. This is also taking stock of yourself, making sure you have everything in check before you head out to face whatever cruel and evil things await. Visit a store for potions if you must, clean your gear, and make sure it matters enough for you to persevere no matter who pressures you.

You would be amazed how many players do not even think about this at all and spend many cycles of their runtime just focusing on what's in front of them, always pushing forward without preparing for what is going to happen. They might think that they can do it again later, that they can restart the whole thing. But in life, you have one life, one adventure at a time, and we are here to do the best we can with the time we are given. A great player (Game Designer) plans, organizes, stocks up on gear, talks to locals for more information, and might even take on some crappy side missions for a few extra coins to get that last piece of gear before they leave. It doesn't matter if you happen to be a novice or a veteran at this game. Every game will be different, which forces you to be nimble in your choices, make the right calls, and live with them.

Now, as you walk to the city gates a guard orders the drawbridge down with the portcullis raised. Your character is given a shield to protect yourself against the onslaught of the adventure in games development. This shield is knowing you have prepared yourself to the best of your ability, and it unlocks the next level, known as Blue Sky. Time to go face those levels. They aren't going to conquer themselves, and the call to glory cannot be ignored. The game awaits.

PREPARATION DEFINITION

The Point

Preparation is your best friend and something to learn as the first step of any journey. Most people think you start the race when the gun fires and you sprint to the finish line. Well, it's time to understand that the beginning happens before any race ever starts.

Further Definition

Preparation itself comes in two forms: mental and informational. Both have their place and should be respected as you get yourself prepared for the great adventure that awaits you. These two areas will get you ready before the game development has begun.

First off, there is mental preparation, which comes in the form of gearing yourself up for the herculean challenge of taking on the game project. You have to decide that you are ready to spend countless hours on a single game, use up all of your creativity daily to where you won't have anything left for hobbies, and be pushed mentally through exhaustion to the point where you might think you're going insane. All of these possible negative points aside, you need to know the positives too. You have to come to grips with the fact that you will be creating digital art that will be enjoyed across the world, you will bond closer with your fellow developers more than any traditional job, and in the end there will be a physical (or digital) copy of all your hard work for that period of your life.

For the informational side, it's good to understand that the process of creating a video game is called a development cycle. That cycle is broken into different phases that make up the whole. Like a level of a video game, you must go through each cycle to get to the boss at the end of each level. If you conquer the boss, you get to go to the next level until eventually everything is completed. Now, to be fair, no two projects are exactly the same. Hell, even yearly iterative titles never really have the exact same scheduling. But all of them have these development/release periods, even if some only last a day. These periods consist of Preparation, Blue Sky, Preproduction, Production, Alpha, Beta, Final, Patch, and Live—all of which I will explain in this book.

Steps to Success

- Take a deep breath and realize that the first step is the mental one where you decide that you are going to work your hardest to complete the game. As practice, select a book you want to read and finish it. (Dangle over the edge of a volcano while you read if you want to up the difficulty.) Learn how to finish.
- Realize that the development cycle is the system you're in. Everyone is in a system of work, life, and connection. Chart out the system you live in daily and see how it works for or against you.
- Learn the art of preparation. The next time you are going to go out, set up a plan for your adventure and follow that system to completion.

PREPARATION: THE QUEST

The Point

Like a knight, you are now charged with a quest: to complete a game. Do you feel ready for that? I thought not. No one ever does, so be prepared for that. If you do, it proves you're not ready for this quest, as you have next to no idea what you're getting into.

Further Definition

I know it's not good to start off by telling the hero (that's you) that they don't know what they are doing. But it serves a very important purpose, which is to allow you to start with a fresh, unfiltered viewpoint (unfiltered pictures are what they will be looking for in a hundred years to see how people lived now). The old adage that the fool and the master are the closest to each other is very true, compared to the student, who is in the massive process of learning. The best thing you can focus on to start off this mission as the fool is a sense of wonderment and joy. Ah, blissful unawareness.

Because you are reading this book, I suspect you're on (or are going to be on) a mission to make a game, which is commendable, as it's a great quest to spend your life on. That said, video game design is not for everyone, and as you move through this book you might discover it isn't something you wish to do. There is no disrespect in making this call. The best we can each do in this life is find what makes us shine and then do that every single day. I have seen many a fine person think they could handle the job, only to burn themselves out in their first outing. Never forget that your survival is the most important part of this mission. Games will be made with or without you.

Lastly, you need to know—not *think*, but truly *know*—what type of hero/heroine you are going to be for this journey. Many people don't think like this when joining on with a game company and are stuck in being who they think they are. Sounds like I'm telling you to put on a mask at work, but that's very much incorrect. What I am describing is that you make a conscious choice to be a better person than you are in your daily life when you are creating a game. This better person will do wonderful and terrible things to everyone around you, which means the least you can do is put some thought into what you want to project to the people in your work life. Remember, it's not about being ultra-good or wickedly evil, as it's your choice to find yourself in the gray area in between. You'd be shocked how many people don't do this before they begin their quests in life.

Steps to Success

- Select any topic you don't know about yet, and spend some time learning just for the sake of learning. Be the fool and teach yourself.
- When looking up your topic of choice, beware of documents, books, or articles that lead you astray. Learn to drop them, as you never want to go all the way down the rabbit hole.
- The first game you play that gives you the choice of good vs. evil, chose one side completely. Without commitment, you suffer from not getting the full experience.

PREPARATION: YOUR CREW

The Point

Every company or group making a game is different, which means it's on you to figure out how the group functions. The better the crew, the better your game will be, as everyone will be pulling in the same direction.

Further Definition

Every game has a different makeup of who works to create it, and you need to understand where the power is. As you are starting off with any group, learn the strengths and weaknesses of the people involved. Coupled with this, you need to learn which people truly hold the power of the project's course. They are the captains, who must be respected even when you disagree with them. The faster you realize who pulls the strings, the better you will be able to help them succeed, as no game is on the designer's shoulders, no matter how much they think it is.

Like most project areas, you can quantify your crew, break it down, and use it to your advantage if you are thinking the right way. It just takes a perception change from you to see things in a different light. To break it down, first take all of the groups you work with and compartmentalize them into their base emotional components. These groups are Owners (ego and company preservation), Producers (mix of emotions and logic), Designers (problem solvers with a god complex), Software Engineers (logic and order), Artists (emotions and beauty), Marketing (emotions and numbers), Operations (stability and consistency), and Quality Assurance (quality and stability). Next, figure out where the power hierarchy is in each group, as there are always leaders with many followers. Then, take the people you most connect with and figure out what they are specifically like, what makes them tick, and what they are passionate about. Sometimes this is as easy as sitting back in a social occasion and just letting them speak about themselves. Finding out what makes someone shine and then letting them talk about it—with you being an active listener—is the easiest way to have anyone become a valued friend.

You need to understand that people make a game as a collective but with a power hierarchy. Within each group there is a power base that in turn rolls up to the next level until you've met the top.

Steps to Success

- Break down each team you work with and figure out the chain of command in each group. Identify the positives and negatives of each member along with how best to communicate with them.
- Analyze the leaders in your game company and write down how best to communicate with each, adding notes for likes and dislikes.
- Start building trust bridges by communicating with the leaders and followers, as both groups have power in a game. You need to learn to utilize them all like a trusty pack of supplies that will get you through this journey.

PREPARATION: YOUR ENVIRONMENT

The Point

Your environment and making it work for you is just as important as coming to grips with creating a game mentally.

Further Definition

Your environment is broken into work, travel, and home. Having each of these optimized can mean the difference between a healthy work/life balance and an emotional husk of a person begging for a quick death.

For work, you will live in a desk. Yes, in, on, around, and even some dark nights sleeping under. (Don't laugh, it happens way too much.) Make your work desk world a pleasant one that makes you happy to come visit every day. Some developers cover their desks with toys, geeky pictures, and symbols of their profession, and for many this is a random collection that grows over time. Instead, what I'm suggesting you do is create a plan to make your workspace a positive place that brings you joy when there is none to be had elsewhere. This plan can include how you select text, pictures, and objects that help you be happy as you will spend countless hours there. Have a theory before the application.

For travel, you must understand that the travel time between office and home needs to be reduced as much as possible. A reduced travel time allows you more time to recharge after work and will allow you that little extra time in the morning to gain rest. (This is worth more than money as far as I'm concerned.) That said, your home should also be close to amenities so you can easily take care of errands—again, this will reduce your travel time so you can start relaxing properly. Whatever you can do to streamline this will allow you to better concentrate on work and on your life when it's needed. Time is valuable and yours is doubly so.

Finally, it's good to keep your home in a state that is easy to manage, a calm and pleasant place that allows you to fully recharge. That means no unneeded clutter (I say toss it out now—less need to care for it or dust it). Creating a cozy space to relax for any hobby is a requirement. Your bedroom should be a peaceful place where nothing will prevent you from getting the rest you need to survive. If you have chores to maintain your world, reduce them to the minimum required to allow you more time to focus on you. Hearth and home is one of my largest requirements in life, as no matter what the world throws at me, I can power back up at home—which I would like you to focus on too.

Steps to Success

- Plan out what would be best on your desk to make you happy. Select three items.
- Find better and faster ways to get home and implement one into your travels.
- That box of junk (we all have at least one) you are holding on to, take it out and toss it into the closest garbage can. Feel better?

CHAPTER 2

Blue Sky

CONTENTS

Level 2: Blue Sky 12
Blue Sky Definition 14
Blue Sky: Core Idea 16
Blue Sky: Research 17
Blue Sky: Shoot for the Moon 18
Blue Sky: Ideas Are Yours or Theirs 19
Blue Sky: Break It Down, Break It Down, Break It Down 21
Blue Sky: Theory vs. Practical 22
Blue Sky: Vision 24
Blue Sky: Don't Be at Home for Fear 25
Blue Sky: Choose a Color Scheme 27
Blue Sky: Possibilities and Solutions 28
Blue Sky: Replay-ability 29
Blue Sky: To Story or Not to Story 31
Blue Sky: Target Audience 32
Blue Sky: Design Is Not Just in Games—Look Outside 33

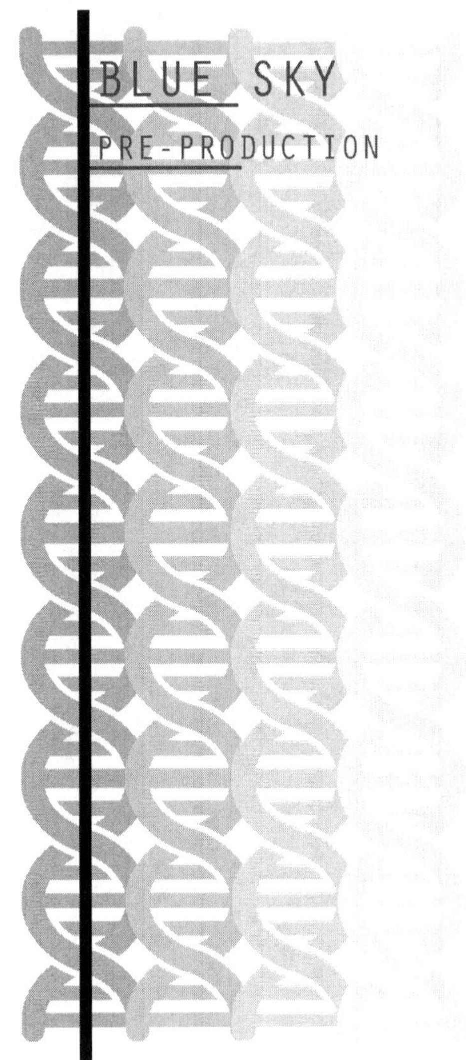

LEVEL 2: BLUE SKY

Now you find yourself on the first leg of this journey with the bountiful blue sky above you. It looks like it goes on forever, and you really haven't figured out if you're in an open world or a game on rails that will get you to the end. You will have to decide that for yourself, and if I do say so, a good mix of both never goes astray. This is a true statement: you may be a participant in this game, but you also have the power to change it to your requirements. Then suddenly you realize you're in a choose-your-own-adventure title allows you to make calls that will lead you through a story to the end. How cool is that?

Now, as you're never alone in the development cycle of a game (or at least, it's extremely rare to be alone), you are surrounded by allies, and at this level it's best to figure out who is out for you, for the game, for the company, or for themselves. They all have different motivations that at times may seem like they are working for or against you to get done what needs getting done. The best part is that these are not enemies. They are just complicated puzzles for you to crack with the proper combination for the betterment of the team and the game.

Unlike the beginning of the game, which is safe and generally very you-centric, you are now in a boundless expanse filled with enemies in every form you can think of. Now adversaries can come out of nowhere to knock you on your ass. Monsters with terrible names like Writer's Block, Complexity, and Visionless will appear out of nowhere, hell-bent on doing everything they can to stop you from reaching the next level. The best you can do is try to handle them and the others one at a time, collect the treasure they drop, moving on to the next as they can all be defeated given the right character.

If enemies were not enough, you will also have to deal with obstacles you never thought could spring up to make you jump and double-jump to avoid. These obstacles take the form of allies' opinions that stalk your every move, problems without solutions that seek to drag you down, and lack of imagination that can strip your armor bare, leaving you quite vulnerable. You know these areas are facts that exist in every game (job). And just because you're in this game doesn't mean you're alone in dealing with them, which means the best you can hope for when finding an obstacle that you cannot power-jump over is that you can call on an ally to help you complete the obstacle.

This is the first occasion where you are presented with the horror of possibly being swallowed alive inside the belly of a beast far larger than you want to understand. This beast will be in your baffles for the whole game, and all I can say is that you need to learn to not be swallowed. Keep the beast where it belongs—behind you—and if it doesn't drive you forward, it's chasing you. It's not your fault you make an attractive snack. If you're lucky (not all are), you'll get some armor that you can use to protect yourself throughout the game. The actions you take here will help you survive the adventure, which means the plates in your armor had better be amazing. This armor allows you into the next level: preproduction.

BLUE SKY DEFINITION

The Point

First off, I will define Blue Sky for you. The second period of a project cycle is called Blue Sky (or high concept, or many other terms to mean the same thing). This is where the ideas are born. If you're wondering about the naming convention, just look up at the sky on a beautiful day and realize that it's limitless in scope, just like your imagination should be for any game. Nothing is off the table.

Further Definition

During this period, a designer will be asked to produce a boatload of preliminary design for the product they are working on through the use of imagination. Brainstorming and communication with other people are key. This idea period is the blueprint for the entire project to follow, and it can draw inspiration from anywhere. It is important and must be respected by you and everyone else in the team, as this will create a course for the game you will be building. Think of it like a blueprint for a building that will one day tower above the masses as a symbol of greatness. It all started with a blueprint.

You need to remember that the design at its core is developed here, and if you don't think big from the beginning your game is already destined for the discount pile. (The first game I worked on that I saw in a bargain bin still haunts me to this day.) I personally call this phase Blue Sky as a reminder to forget everything that limits the fantastical and stops me from looking up at the boundless blue sky above me and creating amazing things.

This is a crucial phase for the project, but it's often rushed through as everyone is more interested in getting on with the game. Just learn to respect your Blue Sky period, as it might be a long time before it comes again. If necessary, take your own time to think it all through, collecting greatness while you can. This is not the only creative period a designer has, but it's about the most unfettered.

Steps to Success

- Start thinking with a mind unclouded by rules. As an exercise, write down all of the ways you can get home today—all of them, no matter how crazy. Everything is allowed, especially jet packs. See how far you can push your imagination.

- Focus on something that makes you angry and think back to the first time it really affected you. Realize that it doesn't affect you now and that you have power over that feeling. The more you learn about yourself and the world, the more likely you will be to think outside of the box.

- Break out of the box you are in. (You are in one. It's okay. Just realize it.) As a simple exercise, try a food that you would never normally try to eat. Simple and silly, I know, but the smallest steps start you on a path to open your mind.

BLUE SKY: CORE IDEA

The Point

At the beginning of every game is the core idea for the product. Whatever you want to call it (one-liner, core, X, razor, key, pitch, etc.), at the heart of a game is the sales pitch. Why does this game exist? Or why should it exist?

Further Definition

This in and of itself sounds really easy, but I've watched people spend months figuring this out for a game. You really have to take what is spectacular about the product, being as specific as you can but leaving enough room for the person who hears it to create their own fantasy.

From the beginning of games, every form of pitch has been created to get the people who control the money to believe this is the best thing since sliced bread (sliced bread having been created last year by you after countless years of scientific experimentation). My favorite term for this is "elevator pitch." Any designer should be able to present the soul of the game in a phrase, sentence, or paragraph in the time it takes to travel to a destination in an elevator. Really, the goal is to get the other person sold on the concept in as few words as possible, allowing them to fill in the gaps. The words, "SHIT, I want to play that game!" should be the level you are trying to get to. If you didn't get a response along those lines, you have to go back to the drawing board to prepare it again for some other hapless redshirt in the next elevator.

No matter what level of designer you are, you should have this skill down to a science that you gently put to sleep every night with warm milk. (Yes, Science loves warm milk. I've checked.) One quote I heard from somewhere that fits this point is, "The greatest designer in the room is not the person with all of the best ideas or the greatest experience or even technical know-how. They are the person who can tell a story better than anyone else in that room."

Steps to Success

- Write five pitches for the game you are working on and try them out on people in your life to see which one works best.
- Take the three that worked the best and cut them down even further. Pitch them again to someone new, someone outside of your regular life, yet still an acquaintance.

- Finally, figure out which one is the best pitch, and simply ask a stranger on the street if they would like to play the video game based on your pitch alone. Repeat more times than you can remember, and you will become a master at this, even if random strangers might think you very odd.

BLUE SKY: RESEARCH

The Point

I cannot stress highly enough that research is your best tool and greatest ally. Any time spent on researching a topic you are working on will expand your understanding of the topic and make sure you are not limited by your preconceived ideas. You think that's air you're breathing … hmm.

Further Definition

Remember to say this out loud constantly: "Research is your best friend." Say it out loud three times now—I can wait. It cannot be stressed enough that doing more research is a best practice for any designer. The more you know, the better you can put it into a game.

There are two main veins of research. One is broad data collection on every possible related topic. This should be a lifetime pursuit for a designer and something you never stop doing at any point. The more well-rounded you are, the better designer you will be. The second is the specific research of games that are similar to the one you are making. Many designers in the past have created great and horrible things that you can learn from.

Spend some time collecting resources from the written word, web pages, pictures, movies, television, music, books, real-life locations, and life events, then get to know them all intimately. Once you feel that you have mastered the real-world elements around the topic you are working on, turn your search to other games that might aid you.

To start, learn about the genre (past products). Figuring out the top twenty badly reviewed items of games in that genre or franchise will show you what not to do and what you could improve. Other people's failure can be your success, and they have already laid it out for you. As well, look at the top twenty amazing items in that genre or franchise and figure how they could be made even better. No one is perfect, everything can be improved upon … chant this three times and repeat nightly.

Personally, I take the research I find and cover my desk, cubicle, and any other spare space I can find in the office with everything to keep it present. Seeing it everywhere helps it creep into your brain when you're not even thinking about it, and it can trigger amazing moments of epiphany. This will also aid you because the information will stay visually present in your life instead of being left in a file someplace you never look.

Steps to Success

- Select a game of a specific genre and collect the top twenty mistakes and great ideas made by other games in the last five years.
- Find at least three movies, websites, or books that are geared toward the genre you're researching and devour them as if there will be a test later.
- Have a friend who knows the source material quiz you to test your memory.

BLUE SKY: SHOOT FOR THE MOON

The Point

One of my favorite sayings is "Always shoot for the moon, because even getting out of the atmosphere is a success." Think, say, and act big at the beginning of the Blue Sky sessions. This is really the point where the ideas are being created that will make a fantastic game.

Further Definition

Even if every idea doesn't reach its greatest potential, it is your responsibility to try. As a designer, it's your job to think so far out of your box that your box currently resides in Alpha Centauri having tea and crumpets. (If you can't imagine that, you need to stop and think about it right now: box, Alpha Centauri, tea, crumpets.)

Designers are the shapers of imagination itself for a massive portion of the population—more games are sold than movies, books, or music. This means we have to step up our game and think bigger than anyone else alive today. That's not an arrogant statement—it's a call to arms. If you have ten robots in your game, then why not one hundred robots? And if one hundred, then why not an intergalactic civilization of robots spanning fifty millennia with a population size of seventeen trillion? Get the "bigger" picture now.

Designers get really mired in the limitations of engines, platforms, and team sizes. All of these concerns can limit your imagination, putting you back into that box in Alpha Centauri (yet strangely, the tea and crumpets are now missing). Your imagination should have no limits and your design doubly so. The best thing you can do is think big and scale it back when it's needed.

Knowing those limitations can make you a better designer as long as you don't lose the big picture. Many a fine designer has lost their way in the fields of limitation. If you ever doubt this, go to any game store and find the bargain bin. That's where limitation lies as someone once used their limited imagination and the bargain bin was where it got them. Lack of thinking big is almost always the cause of most of those poor unfortunate titles that you need to learn from. No matter what ideas get cut down, resized, and retooled throughout a project, it's imperative you create with eyes unclouded. Start massive and then alter to meet the needs of the game when called for—and not before then.

Steps to Success

- Make a game about a fish and then create ten massively outlandish features for the game. Many fine games have been created about fishes.
- Take each of those ten ideas and make then even more creative. Everything can be bigger, greater, and more spectacular if you imagine it. And you need to understand you can make them bigger.
- Now take one idea and blast it out completely. Yes, I know you did your best with the last three, but try harder. I want to see your fish eating those crumpets and drinking that tea.

BLUE SKY: IDEAS ARE YOURS OR THEIRS

The Point

Ideas are dime a dozen and come from everyone who has the guts to speak their mind. You have to learn that not all ideas are equal, right, and good for the game. Check your ego at the door. If you learn to do this, you will be a better designer. Hold on tightly, let go lightly.

Further Definition

Everyone has ideas about what will make a game amazing, and by everyone, I mean every freaking person who finds out you design games. Sometimes I flat out lie when I meet strangers, telling them I work as a cashier in a supermarket, just so I don't have to have the chat about what they think about games. Everyone thinks they know what would make a great game, but few understand that you need to see the masses instead of the individual needs of the player.

Inside a game company, it's even worse. Everyone from tester to CEO believes that their ideas are the best. They have not checked their egos at the door. As a designer, your job is to not only learn to work with their ideas but to accept that yours might not be the best on the table. On many occasions, your ideas can and will take a back seat to people with more power or better concepts. With that said, you need to find a place where collecting all ideas without bias becomes your mantra, and you start judging every concept on its own merit from your experience rather than on who it comes from.

Most people who start off in design want to make their mark as big as possible as fast as possible. Toss out the idea that "you" will be making the game. Realize that it takes a village or a crew on a mission together to make great games. If you let your ego go, you will be much more interested in the collaborative team effort to help make the game better rather than putting your stamp on it, which has destroyed many games over the years.

This is especially important when you end up working on ideas that you had nothing to do with. If this is ever the case, be smart from the beginning and go directly to the person who originally came up with the concept. Strip-mine their brain for every bit of information that can help you make the design amazing, as they have the vision.

Steps to Success

- Make a list of everyone's ideas for your game, no matter who they are, with yours included. Grade them between 1 and 10 … dispassionately. It's easier said than done.
- Take the top five ideas from that list with only one of yours (it hopefully made it into the top five), and get someone else to grade them dispassionately.

- Take the top three and choose the best idea, which is now the basis for your game idea and must be utilized no matter what you think of it. Welcome to games and your lack of control, which is a good thing for anyone to understand.

BLUE SKY: BREAK IT DOWN, BREAK IT DOWN, BREAK IT DOWN

The Point

Every single game starts off with a simple premise or title. From there the designer has to dissect the product into smaller, manageable pieces so they can start getting a handle on the total assets needed to complete the whole. We break it down so that we can build it properly.

Further Definition

Thinking about it like a pyramid with the title or premise at the top, the next levels broken down between the front end (menus) and the back end (gameplay) to fill in the entire pyramid.

Front-end levels are broken into visual screens, the levels farther below are for mechanics and navigation (what the screen does and how one moves through it), and finally, player interaction with those screens at the base of the pyramid.

Back-end levels are broken into major gameplay features (important parts of the gameplay experience) with those mechanics (the parts that go into the feature and environments) and finally at the base of the pyramid the submechanics (the smaller pieces that go into mechanics and levels that make up the experience).

The faster you learn to break things down, the better designer you will be and the easier it will be for your head to remember every single area rather than the massive whole. Games are made by teams, which means no one person truly knows every part of the game, but as a designer it's your job to know more than everyone else.

For many years, no matter what position I was in I spent a massive amount of time learning everything I could to understand the whole on every game I worked on. It's a great learning exercise, and if you can keep the whole product in your head, it will make you indispensable to everyone as you can recall any area in your mind and know what went into it. On more than one occasion because I refused to stop playing the title

I managed to gain an understanding that had executive producers calling me on Sunday morning (my only day to sleep in) to get my advice on how to fix a final hindering bug. I could explain how best to fix it along with all of the possible knock-on issues that might come up, all while sleep deprived and without the game in front of me.

Steps to Success

- Select one of your favorite games, break it down using the pyramid system, filling in all of the points above with the actual information. Reverse-engineer it.
- Take a single gameplay feature and break it down to its mechanics and submechanics, writing them all down in point form to learn more about it.
- Take a day in your life, writing out all of the levels of the pyramid in point form. Start with your name at the top, then waking and sleeping below, and so on.

BLUE SKY: THEORY VS. PRACTICAL

The Point

The first and best debate by designers is theory of design versus the practical application of design. Both have their place, which means you need to learn to balance them as the project continues.

Further Definition

Theory versus practical has been and always will be a sticking point between designers. Every designer has their own certain mix between the two. Old-schoolers will scream that without theory there is no game, while new-schoolers explain that due to years of applicational learning through games, the theory is secondary to getting into the guts of something to make it better through tuning. Both are right, which is why they fight.

Most of the time, designers start with theory and end up in practical just to get the game on the shelves. As the beginning of the project affords time to think out issues and pontificate about what is the best course of action, it's normally ruled by theory. Plus, often the designer just doesn't have anything tangible to tune, so practical disappears like a puff of smoke. As time goes on and more of the game is built, the designer now can see what their design has wrought, allowing them to take that and tune it. This is when practical is much more the house god, and theory is for the documents currently collecting dust in the corner.

Don't get me wrong—there is always a place for theory throughout the project, and having a thought behind the thinker is something that should be present in every designer's mind. What you need to realize is that one feeds the other, and they should never actually be at odds. Unfortunately, I have seen too many designers be one or the other, and the games they worked on suffered because of it. The theory designer has all the deep thought about how the design should work out. They then make a design that when implemented sticks rigidly to the theory even if it doesn't work out. On the other side of the coin, you have the practical designer who spends little time on the thought, bangs out a design to be implemented, and then tweaks the crap out of it when they have it to look at. One wants to be a hero, and the other wants to be the villain. The problem is: both heroes and villains fail. The ones in the middle who learn to balance the two roles survive to old age to tell the tale. Most stories don't go into that point, as it's easier to have one or the other win in the end, which is not what life is about. Designers need to be the antihero archetype, creating their own code of morals to lead their lives melding the theory with the practical to make great, entertaining games.

Steps to Success

- Think about how you will get out of the building you're in. Now write that down in every form of complexity to perform the task in detail. Follow the instructions.
- On a different page, mark down all of the times you didn't follow your instructions or had to change them.
- Hand a version to someone else and have them follow it. How did they do it?

BLUE SKY: VISION

The Point

Vision is quite possibly the most important trait to have as a designer. A vision is the experience of seeing something that other people cannot see and being able to write or talk about it for a game. You need to envision the end result without physically seeing it, and at the same time not be tied to that vision. Tricky business.

Further Definition

Spend time in your own mind figuring out how the game is going to look, sound, act, and play to everyone. This is what is going to help you really achieve success as a designer.

That said, you would be amazed how many people do not have a clear vision for the game they are making and when pushed on the specifics they can't answer you properly. On many occasions, I have seen great men and women crumble in a meeting when they were asked too many specifics. This is because a lack of vision and imagination on their part comes down to the simple statement, "I need to see it in the game before I can make a judgment on my own thought pattern." Yes, that's right—the old chicken-and-egg problem arises, which can cost a game everything.

Personally, having a vision is the very first thing I judge a designer on. If they fail to show the ability they typically don't last long in the games industry. They are tourists. A sad but true statement is that people lacking vision are lacking because they have already forgotten how to play. In my mind, the real test of vision is someone who needs to be told to shut up because they can't stop describing *every* detail without being prompted. They have spent so much personal thought on every detail they can literally see, hear, and feel it in their imagination. When you were a child, you imagined everything around you, creating a vision for your playtime. As we get older, we forget to play, which eliminates imagination. People escape into other worlds like games to recapture that wonderment again. As corny as it sounds, don't stop dreaming!

Steps to Success

- Close your eyes and use your imagination to create a valley in every detail. See it clearly. Now imagine you're walking through this valley with a companion. Visualize that companion. Now suddenly you are attacked. Visualize the entire encounter, finally succeeding in the encounter and coming out of the valley. Congratulations, you just thought up a vision for a game level.
- Close your eyes and use your imagination to create any location in your mind. Now add in all the objects, the time of day, any inhabitants, structures, and any weather effects you desire. Congratulations, you have the environment for a game.
- Close your eyes and use your imagination to create a hero. What do they look like? What clothing are they wearing? Why are they a hero? What is their backstory? Congratulations, you have just created a vision for a character in a game.

BLUE SKY: DON'T BE AT HOME FOR FEAR

The Point

Fear to create can be the worst deterrent to creativity. You need to overcome your own fears before creating.

Further Definition

You are not the sum of your fears and as such should not be a home for them, allowing them to drive your actions. This is a positive, forward-thinking statement, but it can be the opposite of the way you lead your life. Fear drives the best of us to run, seek comfort in what we know, and shun others as well as new ideas for the safety of the known. The known is a cozy blanket we can pull up over our eyes when the monster comes out from under our beds to devour us whole.

First of all, you need to accept that everyone has fears and that's okay. Once you know that and know you're not alone, you can start to figure out how best to understand your fears. I always find it best to name my fears, as it gives me a focus to look at going forward. And yes, sometimes my fears get silly names to denote how ridiculous they are and yet they still scare me. (You know what you've done, Engelbert. I'm watching you.) Next, I try to put myself in a calm place in my world and think back to the first time I ever felt the fear. Sometimes this involves going way back to my youth, and other times it's something new that cropped up last week. Once I have identified the root cause, I try to think up what I can do to thwart the fear. What positive action can I do to get myself out of that fear? Fear is the cousin of laziness, which means it runs scared at the sight of action. If the fear cannot be conquered in a day, then spend days or weeks focusing every day on what you can do to conquer it and acting on that. Eventually you will rob the fear of its power and bring yourself back to be a better designer.

I mention this with design because with most creative endeavors there is a hint of fear behind every decision. This fear is a product of our previous choices. We learn from our mistakes or are supposed to. Sometimes our fears scare us into inaction, and other times they drive us to not make any call on a design decision at all, which is always worse. You need to be one with your fears and look to them for support when you need it to make the right call on your decisions.

Every day I'm alive I fight with my fears, my misconceptions, and the outright lies that I have told myself. It's hard and often filled with difficult choices about what I believe. Some days I win, and I get home to celebrate a day well fought. Some days I crawl home totally defeated to lick my many wounds. The key for me is to try every day and not carry any wounds forward after the day they are felt. If I want to get on with my life, I have to be driven to letting my fears go instead of letting them control me. You can do the same, and I can tell you that a designer who understands their fears is far more profitable than the one who runs from them.

Steps to Success

- Take any fear you have, name it, and figure out where it came from.
- Think up three positive actions daily to conquer your fear.
- Document when you have conquered your fear. List your wins.

BLUE SKY: CHOOSE A COLOR SCHEME

The Point

You might think that color choice is in the hands of the art team, but when you're preparing a game idea it's important to decide on a color palette to help the idea come to life.

Further Explanation

Color evokes emotion, and the combination of colors can help convey the feelings behind your design to everyone in the Blue Sky period. This means you need to decide on a set of colors that will be integral to your game. You might think this will be easy to do, but there are a lot of complexities involved in coming to a solid decision.

To begin with, it's good to investigate gender complexities, as the sexes see colors differently. Men prefer to see cooler colors that dominate in the blue/green range, while women tend to gravitate toward warmer colors in the red/orange range. Location will also affect their choices, as people in warmer climates focus on warmer colors and the inverse is true for the colder climates.

Next, it's good to look at cultural complexities, as not every country interprets colors the same way. Many color facts you have grown up with will be called into question, and you must investigate the dominant countries where you want to sell your game to come up with colors that best appeal to your game audience rather than repulse them. A purple-dominated palette can seem completely different to someone in Europe and someone in South America. The more you begin to understand that the colors you choose are international, the better you will be able to connect with your audience.

Lastly, look at the class complexities, which take the form of base colors versus gradient colors. Lower-class to middle-class gamers tend to gravitate to base colors, and middle to upper classes prefer gradient choices in their color spectrum. On one occasion I had an art director put a color scheme together for a game that used different gradients to get his message across. When I asked the designers who were in the target market for the game if it appealed to them, not one liked it. The art director was appealing to the production house and senior developers, yet had forgotten the core demographic who would buy the game. After many discussions, the change was made to bring it back to base colors, and it had the automatic effect of appealing to the target market again. We did a test, bringing in outside help to see which presentation would connect with the target market, and the base color worked every time. Lesson learned and one you should learn.

In the end, you need to come up with three to five colors that fit best for your game and use them to tie the product together. Good luck.

Steps to Success

- Research different color theory options for gender.
- Select any base color and research how various continents and countries see that color.
- Look up brands that use base colors versus gradient colors.

BLUE SKY: POSSIBILITIES AND SOLUTIONS

The Point

Designers provide solutions to problems, not the other way around. No matter how mad the solution is, they have one (or three) ready for every single situation. This is done by filtering through all of their accumulated experience with the product (and everything else they have ever learned) to offer the most elegant way to sort out the issue.

Further Definition

In the old days, designers started off pretty much in quality assurance (testers), cutting their teeth in the trenches of many projects. Many a fine tester I know has decided to do the daylight charge over the open minefield to try to get into design, but only a few have made it. The fundamental difference between quality assurance and design is this: quality assurance reports problems, and design generates solutions.

In design, your number-one motto should be "I (or we) have a solution." Every single issue you come across should be met with at least three possibilities for solutions to the problem, weighing all the information you currently have at your disposal about the product. (Note: No designer ever has all of the information, so don't worry—just go with what you currently know.)

Now, take a breath. It's important to think things over, and I have found a single breath helps with that, allowing you to let your thoughts become more succinct. When you have generated the possibilities firmly in your mind, offer one verbally that you believe is the best possible route to success, explaining your reasoning for that choice. Even if it's not the solution that is chosen, you now have a method that allows you to back up your reasoning. We all learn from our mistakes, which aids us in giving a better answer next time. The moment you start training yourself to do this in all facets of your work life, the more helpful you will be for every single member of your team. Now take another deep breath, and think about what you have just read.

Steps to Success

- Try for one day to evaluate every problem you have in your life, using the possibilities and solution equation mentioned above. You will find there are too many. Learn to be okay with that.
- For every design issue you run into, actually write down three possibilities for success into your documentation, highlighting your desired solution. Sometimes another solution can be easily implemented later if the first one didn't work.
- Be a positive member of the cult of solutions. Many times the other disciplines will be looking for the designer to have the vision of the final outcome. That means you have to have worked out all of the possible issues already in your head: I see it like this, I see it playing like this, the hurdle is dealt with like this, and so on.

BLUE SKY: REPLAY-ABILITY

The Point

If you want your game to be loved and adored, build in the replay-ability right from day one.

Further Explanation

Most (if not all) designers want their game to be played more than once. A single playing experience only scratches the surface of the world they create. Because of this need, many designers build layers of replay-ability into their games to keep players coming back to what is functionally the same offering. At the very beginning of the design process, you should be thinking about how you're going to get players to play the game more than once, from multiple endings to multiplayer and everything in between.

I've made the joke on a few occasions that the cheapest replay-ability is just having two endings the player can get to, which forces them to go through the entire experience again just for the different ending sequence. Don't laugh—it works! But it only doubles the gameplay without offering any real changes. To go to the next level, look at what building blocks are in the product that you can tweak, change, and manipulate to get a different result. Things like turning the levels upside down or changing the time of day can make the world an entirely new adventure. Swapping out enemies or changing the difficulty of enemies with random rewards can keep the player coming back. Use your imagination with the items at hand to build an experience that can be expanded to offer the player something new with the variables of the game they already know. Some of the best offerings I've seen based on single-player games have the ability to go do the levels again with unique modifiers and goals, making it another adventure altogether just using the same level. Building in a multiplayer choice invites replay options, as the players in the various levels and the selected game type can keep people coming back for years after the titles has been launched. For the ultimate replay-ability, I go back to the basics of stand-up arcade game design that focused on quick, punishing gameplay that beckoned you to dump more quarters into the machine. These arcade beauties live or die on replay-ability with the same variables of start slow, build to insanity, and if you want to continue, that will be another quarter.

Now, not all games are built to be played again. Some are built to simply be a single situation experience that is completed and forgotten. This is normally due to time constraints, money pressures, or lack of imagination. This doesn't make it right, it just makes it a necessary evil that brought the game to a "one-shot experience," as I call it. Too many games are like this, which means it's up to you to come up with ways to make your game replayable for the masses.

Steps to Success

- Take a game you love to play constantly and figure out why you keep going back to it. What are its replay-ability qualities?
- Take a classic video game and work out three ways replay-ability can be added to make it an experience to go back to.
- Find an arcade, play many different games, and learn why they draw you back.

BLUE SKY: TO STORY OR NOT TO STORY

The Point

Most games nowadays have a story, but not all games require one. This is where you need to decide if your game is served by having a narrative.

Further Explanation

The straight truth is that games with narratives sell more than those without. The data is there, and it really points to the idea that people fundamentally love stories in the games they play. If they want a passive story, they watch movies, TV, or Internet content. This doesn't mean you have to include a story, but I would suggest looking into it first before you abandon the idea.

The question you should be asking if you have decided to add a story to your game is what level of story is really needed. A full narrative game can be costly in both manpower and time. To begin with, look at the goal of the game. This will lead you back to what level of story is needed. The levels of stories are basically as follows: Story Free (simple premise, no story), Story Added (simple premise with small interludes of story), Story Base (full story with interludes between levels), Story Plus (full story with story decisions and interludes between levels), and Story Full (full story with many story arcs throughout gameplay to feed the full narrative). Now, these are blanket terms for the levels in story games, but most titles fit within this system, which makes it easier to understand once you start. After you have figured out which story version your game falls into, then you can start to figure out what level of story complexity you want to go to. As an example, a Story Base game can have a 2-minute intro to explain to the player what the point of the game is. It could then have 30- to 60-second interludes between "X" number of levels to push the story along, and then a final 2- to 5-minute sequence at the end of the experience to wrap the story up. Within this example, you can now figure out how much interaction dialogue or expository dialog is required to get the player to the next situation. Plus, it's always good to remember that whatever story is added it will need to be localized. This can be an added cost you should look at before going whole hog on the story design. As always, break down your story into smaller parts to serve the greater story arc—it's always easier to deal with it when it's in pieces rather than an entire epic where if you pull at one thread the whole thing unravels.

Some of my favorite game stories over the years have been ones that are simple, straightforward, and serve the game well to keep me attached to playing it. I think this has to do with my desire to enjoy the gameplay itself. In many games, the story can take over the experience, leaving the player bored waiting to get to the next gameplay adventure. I have fallen asleep waiting for a story sequence to finish. Whatever you choose, I just ask that you focus on a story that people will want to know and that aids the game. A story just for story's sake is a waste of time.

Steps to Success

- Pick a game that doesn't have a story and make one up for it.
- Now pick the right level that supports the game.
- Finally, break out everything needed to add that story to the game.

BLUE SKY: TARGET AUDIENCE

The Point

Finding a game's target audience is the delicate art of selecting exactly which players are best suited to enjoy the game. This means finding out who they are, where they are, and how old they are.

Further Definition

Not every game is made for every player. Figuring out your best target audience can take a bit of doing. It's no good having a game that only connects with a small subgroup of the world population, but it's also a failure to think that everyone on the planet will want to play the game.

To break it down, first figure out if your title is meant for both men and women. Not all titles focus on both genders, and routinely many of them stick to a single gender focus. A single gender focus allows you as a designer to specifically work on classic needs of that gender. That isn't to say you *should* focus on just one. I have seen many games fail as they designed themselves into a corner, only thinking about how one group would receive it. Most of the time it's sage advice to think about both genders—or keep it gender-neutral—as that opens up the possibility of bringing everyone to the table.

Next you need to understand the target market you most wish to appeal to. Most designers start off with key large markets that are broken into three areas: North America, Europe, and Asia. These are large blanket areas and the first markets to look toward, as they are the most likely to purchase games. After that, there are smaller, secondary markets around the world, but on the whole you are looking to focus on one, maybe two, of these large markets. Some game companies do get all three and as designers look to expand their reach past their own location. Many games become international successes—not all, but some—which means it's always good to focus on one location first. Especially at the start.

Finally, you will want to figure out the age ranges you are looking for. Players can be grouped into under-18, 18 to 35, 36 to 49, and 50 years and older. If you're making a child-focused game, the under-18 age range is your target as they will be the most likely to play your game. As video games have planted themselves in the modern landscape for 40-plus years, the age of gamers has expanded. When I first started making games, everyone wanted the 18 to 35 market, but as the years have gone by I have seen games focus their offerings to older markets. Whatever age range you focus on, this will be the group you are trying to make media for. Think like the age demographic you're looking to hook.

Steps to Success

- Select any TV show and break out the demographics for it.
- Select any game and work out the key gender, location, and age focus for it. Do some research to find out if your hypothesis was accurate.
- Research games that worked in one location but not in others.

BLUE SKY: DESIGN IS NOT JUST IN GAMES—LOOK OUTSIDE

The Point

At its core, game design is the act of creating another world that someone is going to experience. Knowing as much as you can about games is a great thing, but the real test of a designer is wanting to understand the design of life itself. The world, its history, and where it is going will help you drive great games.

Further Explanation

A tale of two designers will illustrate my point. I had a design director once who had a wealth of experience with any video game. If it was out there, he had sampled it, played it, and knew the best and worst about the game. In other words, his language of design was what games had come out in the past, what was currently popular, and what he foretold would be the best of breed coming up.

Another senior designer I worked with alongside this design director didn't much like playing games and routinely only played two to three titles a year. This designer spent most of his time looking at every discipline of design he could get his hands on, from architecture to fashion. He firmly believed that games had evolved to a closer point of reality, making his language of design life itself.

Needless to say both parties never had a common language to discuss design together, as both of them had taken their discipline to an extreme. In the end, the two parted ways. The design director went off to another company without ever thinking he needed to change, while the senior designer decided he could fill out his portfolio with some more game experience—generously selected from his fellow designers' best-of-show categories. Who do you think will be the sought-after employee in the future? It's not enough to know everything about games to be a game designer. You have to step outside the box you put yourself in when you donned that title of video game designer. Experience what the world has to offer with all design. No great artist, musician, or designer you look up to was satisfied with what already existed. They reinvented it in a way no one had ever thought of before.

Steps to Success

- Get out of your game box! Spend a day selecting a design discipline that has never interested you and researching it. The point is not to like or dislike it but to truly sample what is out there in design. Design is what the world is made of.
- Do this with a different design discipline for one day every week and watch your experience blossom. You might just find you like it!
- Design something from a completely different discipline that you have always found interesting. It doesn't have to compare to the great works of the leaders of that school, you just have to have tried in a practical way. You need to try.

CHAPTER 3

Pre-production

CONTENTS

Level 3: Pre-production 36
Pre-production Definition 38
Pre-production: Duration 40
Pre-production: Design Document 41
Pre-production: Grand Design Document vs. Micro Design Docs 42
Pre-production: Write for Your Audience 44
Pre-production: Prototype or Suffer 45
Pre-production: Backstory 46
Pre-production: Evoking Emotions 48
Pre-production: Three Levels of Complexity 49
Pre-production: Innovation vs. Boilerplate 50
Pre-production: Make a Model 52
Pre-production: Micro Adventures 53
Pre-production: Lights, Camera, Camera 55
Pre-production: Tools—Look to the Future 56
Pre-production: Audio Design 57
Pre-production: Monetization 59
Pre-production: Platform or Platforms 60
Pre-production: Communicate Early 61
Pre-production: Character Growth 63
Pre-production: Controls 64
Pre-production: Diversity 65
Pre-production: Localization 67
Pre-production: Falling Down the Rabbit Hole 68

LEVEL 3: PRE-PRODUCTION

With your adventuring really starting to pick up steam, it's a good time to mention that there is a gate at the end of this level. You better be ready for it, as it's a big one. The knowledge that there will be a test shouldn't dissuade you from meeting it head-on. It's always good to know what's on the horizon, like looking into the distance and there lies a giant door. You know that no matter what happens, you will need to meet it.

In this level, you will face the nega version of yourself (dark you) who will appear to stop you from taking what you have learned and applying it to the specifics by dismembering part of yourself gained in the Blue Sky level. The devil is in the details, and now you'll be forced to fight yourself—and that monster knows all of your moves, which means you need to think outside your skill tree or the gear you're carrying to find a way to vanquish this foe. If it is defeated, you will gain a sword to help you fight any monster.

If you're really lucky, like beaten up with a four-leaf clover lucky, you will have the opportunity to meet a deity (the money people) who will descend from their realm to speak with you about the game. After discourse, debate, or clear cut bribery, you might get their blessing in the form of treasure (funds for developing the game). If you don't have the skills or frittered around in the last level, the deity will just straight-up leave, forcing you back to the beginning. Here's hoping you impress, as this is crucial to getting through the gate.

Finding a dark version of you and meeting a deity are just the big beats of the level, which has all manner of monsters to contend with. All of this has an effect on you that you are not exactly ready for, as your allies will judge you in this level against your deeds to help the team get to the gate. There will be stress; there will be narrow misses and harrowing moments for good or ill. There is a decent amount of defeat in this level, as it can be trial and error to find the right combination to get through it. The game takes its toll, and you will acquire your first scars as you realize that you're part of a larger group that is focused on the singular goal of getting through that gate.

After countless day and night rotations of the game world, you will finally come to the great and impressive gate. To your surprise, there a camp set up to house all of your allies. You didn't even realize that they have all been working in their own way to get here just like you. You can tell that this means a lot to everyone, as they show their own scars like badges of honor around the campfire. For the first time, you don't feel alone in this game. After feasting you all wander up to the altar before the gate, and lay your pieces of the puzzle together until all pieces are present. If you did this correctly, the gate's giant doors open up to show you all a brand new land known as Production, which is cause for celebration after your hard work thus far. If you didn't put all the right puzzle pieces together, the deity is sure to no longer be around to bestow its favor on you. This forces your entire group back to the Blue Sky level or, worst of all, you are all banished back to the beginning. No one ever wants that after this much work.

PRE-PRODUCTION DEFINITION

The Point

The third period of a games cycle is called pre-production. This is where the ideas are being developed and ironed out before production can be met. Think of this as the sketch before the artistic masterpiece can be created.

Further Definition

During pre-pro (games people love buzz terms), a more detailed design document is generated with all of the members of the team chipping in to help get the work done. I cannot stress enough that the design creation should be done as a collaboration with all of the designers and developers, with the lead having the final say. Think benevolent dictatorship. If you do not involve others, you will miss out on their experience and more importantly their buy-in.

This design document specifies the primary goals of the product and tries to establish whether the design is achievable. If the design is not achievable, the design team can make adjustments early in the process to make sure that it is. I personally have seen some great first drafts of design documents that were not even vaguely achievable if you had ten years and a team of three hundred, so don't worry if everything needs to be edited to fit the dates.

It's at this time that all of the other groups seem to hear the imaginary starting gun and get into the boat with you that you have been fashioning up to this point. Coders get involved developing architectural software along with a detailed technical design document based on the design document. (While this is basic, you would be amazed to hear how often it gets left out and is desperately needed.) Artists start to develop visual concepts, preliminary environment buildups, and visual standards documentation that they will use for the product's duration. (Again, games have been made without it and it has hurt them later on.) As well, the producers and project managers look at the entire team's speculated workload based on the documentation and combine it into a project schedule, accessing if the features and mechanics are possible within the timeline. If all goes well during this period (it normally doesn't, but it's your job to roll with it), financing is put in place for the team to move into the production period. This gate must be met to move to the next step of the game. If it's not, you're back to the drawing board.

Steps to Success

- Take some time with one software engineer to learn more about their documentation and process to help you perform your job better. One hour minimum.
- Do the same with an artist to learn more about their documentation and visual process, as it will help you perform your job better. Again, one hour minimum.
- Finally, do this with project managers and producers to learn the project plan as it lays out the roadmap of your journey to final. You need to know their minds to achieve success and help your game succeed.

PRE-PRODUCTION: DURATION

The Point

You have a finite amount of time to complete your game, which means you need to make decisions based on the knowledge that it will come to an end.

Further Definition

There are three elements to this equation: time, money, and quality. These are the cornerstones of any product in project management. With enough time, any group can make a platinum hit, but the reality is that the game has to come out at a certain point to make profit. With enough money, you can have countless staff as well as the best tech to make a platinum hit, but every game has a budget that has a limit. With enough quality, any group can have a platinum hit, but polish comes at a cost to time and money. Every project fits into this triangle with one of the elements at each point.

This means every decision needs to be made with you weighing up the cost against all of the variables that you know. It's a balance between all of them, no matter how much you think one should win out. The best projects are like a juggler keeping all the balls in the air for their performance. It sounds easy, but the calls you make at the beginning of the project when you have all three—time, money, quality—will be very different later on when you have next to none. Making choices early on can save you and your game later. It's just hard to make calls without all of the facts, which requires you to think three steps ahead.

To be clear, you may not be in a position to have an effect on the three points of the triangle. Project managers and producers typically steer the boat to one point more than another. What you should do is stay in the know which way the boat is sailing, which can then aid you in making calls. The more you know about the milestones along with the work that needs to be completed, the more you'll know if your group is about to do a daylight charge over the open minefield. (This would be certain death, in other words.) Plus, you should know that a proper project plan does not and never should account for overtime as an expectation. If you see that on a project plan. The project manager has already failed.

Steps to Success

- Look up a piece of art you want to replicate (select something you can do). Select all of the colors you need, and set a specified time to complete it.

- Now replicate that art. At the 50% mark take away half your colors, and at the 75% mark remove the original piece from your view of reference.
- Realize that if you could look at the piece with unlimited time you could replicate it, with all of the colors you wouldn't have a problem replicating it, and with unlimited time you could do it to perfection. Now look at your test and realize what you had to sacrifice to get the job done. (I totally failed the first time I did this and didn't even finish it)

PRE-PRODUCTION: DESIGN DOCUMENT

The Point

The design document is the greatest treasure to the designer in pre-production and production. This item is clearly your view of how the game is going to be played without having played it yet. Call it the best-case scenario, as it will never be perfect, will suffer from being outdated, and will be fought over more than any other document you will ever write. It's your job to have the thought before the thinker.

Further Definition

This document is the preliminary vision of the product as well the direction that you and the team want to be going in. There are at least three key points that a design document needs. First is a solid format to keep you on track, making it easier for everyone to understand and reference. Second, you need to be clear with every statement, leaving no holes for questions to arise. Third, it needs to be written for everyone from tester to CEO to understand, which is no easy feat.

To my knowledge, these three points of design documentation have NEVER actually happened, so don't expect success. This quote has always made a lot of sense to explain this case: "When I design in my head I'm a genius, but when I speak it out loud I'm a fool." No matter how hard you try, not everyone will read, think, or act like you, which means your design will never hit every mark. The quest is always to try. Be prepared that when you have finished the design document you will have to discuss it at length with everyone, and not everyone is going to agree with it. This means you have to remove your ego from your design the moment it's completed (it's easier said than done, believe me).

You might think your design is an original work of art, but you will need to edit it no matter what, thus bringing your lofty masterpiece down to the level of a gig poster that's been stapled for two years to a telephone pole on the corner of a busy cross-street. Suck it up, princess—life is in the edits. Some of the greatest designers I know understand how to steer the boat through the great waves of chaos that take hold the moment you release that document into the world. Learn that it's your job to ride those waves rather than be at the mercy of them.

Steps to Success

- Beg, borrow, or steal a design document from some game to see how they did it. Then write one similar to that for a game you would like to make, improving on it where you see fit. Use the Internet to find what you can.
- Always finish your designs! Even that little gameplay mechanic document you wrote way back when that didn't go anywhere adds to your portfolio, showing your evolution of design. Keep it all.
- Write a game in one page and realize the limitation of the page. Give that page to a friend with no preface and watch how they react to it to learn how little control you have over the process.

PRE-PRODUCTION: GRAND DESIGN DOCUMENT VS. MICRO DESIGN DOCS

The Point

A grand design document is a single document that has every bit of the design of an entire product inside it. Micro design docs are individual smaller documents for every part of the entire design of the game. Both have their place, which means you need to know how to produce both depending on the company.

Further Definition

There are two main schools of thought about design documentation, and both are correct for the right game. On the one hand, a grand design document that houses all of the design in one place, while massive, is very easy for everyone to search for information. It's a defining holy text that everyone can look to for guidance. But it can be difficult to update for everyone and take a large amount of pre-production time to create. Micro design docs, on the other hand, house the design in multiple documents spread out in a folder system. This allows the design to be handed off when completed in a centralized area for people to access its information. These micro docs can be easily updated but are a little more difficult to search for information (think one book versus a library section).

I personally have done games with both methods, and I have to say that there is no place anymore for the grand design document (GDD). It takes too long to create, update, and actually keep up at the end of the production cycle. Instead, take on the idea of having a link system written into your micro design docs (I always love the phrase "I'd like to push the 'DO YOU WANT TO KNOW MORE' button") that will pop up your other documents that reference that section. Always implement a version control on the documents and update everyone and their dog on a daily basis whenever you make changes, to keep everyone in the loop. Your documents are truly your greatest communication tool for everyone inside and outside the company. The more you have them in order for everyone quickly, the better everyone can create the product. On a side note, you also have to remember that documentation is just a set of directions to help the creators stay on course (kind of like a boat's course to a destination), and no matter what, the documentation will inevitably take a back seat to getting the product done. It's just your job to make sure it stands until it's no longer of use.

Steps to Success

- Take a single feature in your favorite game or one you're working on and write a design document for it in the grand design document format, timing yourself.
- Take another single feature in your favorite game or one you're working on and write multiple design documents for it in the micro design docs format, timing yourself
- How long did it take you to write both? Now that is how long it will be for someone to start creating the game after. You're not a building architect who finishes everything before everyone else can begin, so learn that succinct design early helps build faster.

PRE-PRODUCTION: WRITE FOR YOUR AUDIENCE

The Point

When writing design you need to first think about exactly the audience you are writing for and tailor your language accordingly. Every person is a combination of experiences, which means you need to find some common groupings to specialize your writing style.

Further Definition

Now, not all design needs to be written for all audiences but you should try to as much as possible. Which brings me to the specifics of where your design will be going when it's completed. First of all, you need to understand your audience, which means understanding the people and groups you are creating design for. Poetry has its place, but not so much as dialogue in a murder mystery television series.

Using blanket terms, software engineers need design to be technical/unemotional, artists need it to be visual/emotional, producers and managers need it to be clear/quantifiable, and quality assurance needs to know how it's verifiable. If you are writing a design for an environment, its audience is artists, which means you need to put in as much description, visual details, pictures, and the feelings that you want the player to experience to aid artists in creating a superior level for the product. In the same vein, creating design for a gameplay mechanic will be mostly for a software engineer who needs to know how it will act, its edge conditions, what criteria are needed to achieve its success, and how it fits into the greater scheme of gameplay.

Now, I will admit not all groups of people are the same, so you really need to spend time getting to know your team to find out how they communicate the best. Then write for them, as they are the core audience, with the other groups being a smaller percentage of the audience pie (e.g.: 80% software engineer, 10% artist, 5% producer, 5% tester). The more you get into this and put a percentage marker for each group at the top of the document, the better your design is going to be understood by others. Making your intentions clear can be the greatest aid to your success as everyone is on the same page—no pun intended, just happy coincidence.

Steps to Success

- Using technical terminology, write a definition of a flower. Hand it to someone else without a title and see if they can figure out what it is.

- Verbally describe a sunset to someone else in as much detail as you can and have them draw it without you watching. Did it turn out the way it looked in your head?
- Learn who your audience is for each design and fit each group into a percentage (out of 100% total) to better understand who you're writing for. This is helpful for you *and* for them.

PRE-PRODUCTION: PROTOTYPE OR SUFFER

The Point

Prototype fast, and often to prove out anything in the game that needs to be figured out. The more prototyping you do early, the safer your development will be.

Further Definition

When I first started in games, prototyping was difficult, time consuming, and normally (at best) in a gray world (one three-dimensional floor with a gray background) which could show me very little of what I was looking for in a feature. With the growth of technologies it's a thousand times faster to get something prototyped and see how it works in the game world. I have even seen teams make a call on canceling an idea for a game based on a prototype that was a grand idea on paper but in application was a boring mess. The prototype saved them months of going down the wrong track. It's a great tool to help not only the designer but all the other teams in the development group see what could be.

This means as early as possible work with the other development groups to try out gameplay elements in a prototype. Treat the prototype like a small project with very basic success/failure goals, a short timeline to get it completed, and whatever team members will be needed to build it out. As the prototype is being created you can help steer it to get to the goals set out. In this way you can rapidly come up with what you're looking for or prove what can and cannot be done. This is important for everyone's learning, as possible outcomes can be tested out before everyone goes down a very long road of developing it fully. When time is money and development time doubly so, this is a very sage area to focus on. Plus, the prototype can work not just to prove out ideas but as a sales point for people inside and outside the company to know what you're up to. It's a playable visual for people to sink their teeth into, and on many occasions I have seen people playing with the prototype for pure enjoyment. It's the first taste of what they will be spending their time on.

Now, the place where most designers and companies tend to stumble and fall with prototyping is that they only do it at the beginning. They prove out their theories and then get on with making the game with the lessons they have learned. I'm here to tell you that you should never stop prototyping if given the chance. Advocating for prototyping time while developing, I guarantee you, will help unlock areas you didn't know possible as the development of the game goes on. I've seen this save entire titles as the changes found in a prototype quickly over a week helped the entire development team pivot to better gameplay with minimal changes to the project plan. Work out time in the project schedule for this with other members of the team, and if it's not needed there are always other areas that could use the time to perfect.

Steps to Success

- Take a deck of cards and come up with a new game today.
- Now make some cards of your own to be added to the deck [insert imagination here].
- Now test this game out with a friend. Prototyping 123.

PRE-PRODUCTION: BACKSTORY

The Point

If you want to understand how a story came into being, it's always good to have a backstory that led the story into being in the first place.

Further Definition

Having a backstory is often a forgotten or missing part of designing out a narrative, yet it's still very important to help explain the "why" of the tale. In today's language we call a backstory a "prequel" to the adventure—we see this in books and movies. This starter story explains the world, people, and events that led to the story. Most designers I've met tend to glance over this as a waste of time, but having a backstory is a great way to help explain the story itself.

Many old Icelandic sagas start off multiple generations before the events of the saga's main characters. This backstory explains everything that brought the main characters to the main story. It explains the events that drove their ancestors to create the world they find themselves in now and why they take the actions they do in the story. The sagas teach us all that a well-developed backstory can be of real benefit.

I myself find this exercise very helpful as it fills in the major events of the world and in my own head explains the environment the player will inhabit. Now, it doesn't have to be a massive tome of stories or go on for volumes, it just has to be something that can be called upon to help you as well as any development team members understand the game's world. To achieve this, I first put myself in the world of the story I have drawn up and think of the main events for the last generation that affected the world as a whole. These events I borrow liberally from our own wealth of human history. It's always better to borrow from situations that people understand because they have already occurred, and then give them a twist to make them work with the fictitious world I am generating. Once I have five to ten events, I use that as the skeleton and build out the people who led to the main characters. I add in the events of their lives that affected each of them and a small narrative that explains who they are. This can be done in a few pages and allows you to figure out how everything fits together. Even if this backstory has no effect on the game, it adds information for everyone building the game to understand the narrative.

If you have the time in the development schedule, I suggest trying this out—even if your game is a simple card game, it's a good exercise to come up with why people are playing cards in the first place. The smaller the game, the simpler the story, the easier the backstory is to build, and it will at least shed some light on the world for you.

Steps to Success

- Select a game, come up with three events from history, and add a twist that fits the game world to explain why the game starts.
- Go find a saga and read it to understand a backstory's use.
- Take a simple game and write a one-page backstory for it.

PRE-PRODUCTION: EVOKING EMOTIONS

The Point

We as human beings are a myriad of emotions, and we look for those emotions in our media, which means we need to think like that when designing a game.

Further Definition

Evoking an emotional response from any media is difficult at the best of times when we are so saturated with it to the point of overload in our technological age. That said, it doesn't mean that we shouldn't try to create emotional moments in games. We should be striving to have some form of emotional resonance in the games we build for the players to experience. The only problem is most games forget that and go for the base levels instead of seeking emotional depth.

But how, you ask, am I the designer supposed to add emotions to a game when the primary throughput is fun? Well, this is where you are wrong. As games evolve, so too should the thought behind the creation of them. It requires you the designer to think outside the box you have normally been given with your media education and start to come up with the primary, secondary, and tertiary emotions you want the player to come away with from the game.

First, this takes the form of coming up with the primary emotion (e.g.: pride) that will be your guiding light for the product. Ask yourself what emotion best suits the game. Spend a decent amount of time coming up with this emotion—as you develop the game it will be a guiding star for all. Second, you should break the game into sections like acts of a play and come up with emotions that best suit those sections. These are the secondary emotions that complement the primary emotion (e.g.: inspiration and hope). Even if it's not a story-based game you should be dividing it up into parts that each have an emotional point. Every game has ups and downs just like the emotions of people, which means you need to plan for it. For the third level down, think of the tertiary emotions (e.g.: gratitude, serenity, and awe) for each section that will fold up to the secondary emotions which complement the primary emotion. These micro emotions can even be level-based. I've played many a game that was seeking to make me feel a different emotional journey on my way to the end of its level, which than changed massively in the next level.

The trap you have to avoid, though, is making your game one note emotionally, as that will doom it to the sales rack, and people being much savvier with their media these days will see right through it. Adding emotional variety is more difficult than you might imagine and is constantly left out in favor of the blanket term I've heard more than I care to say, which is "Make it fun." That is one note, normally uttered by people with as much emotional depth as a wet paper bag. You're better than that, which means the design you create should be better than that.

Steps to Success

- Select a favorite game and come up with its primary emotion.
- Read a fiction book and break it up into the three to five secondary emotions that you experienced from reading it.
- Select any game with many levels to it, play through each, and chart the emotions you come away with for each as you get to the end of the game.

PRE-PRODUCTION: THREE LEVELS OF COMPLEXITY

The Point

Start to think about every part of your design as having three levels of implementation. Not everything you design will make it into the final product. This method of thought will teach you to think about your design's implementation into the product if everything cannot be created.

Further Explanation

The Good, the Bad, and the Ugly is a design philosophy that has many different names, but I like this one the best. I have seen this formulation of design have tremendous success in games and aid the entire production from start to finish.

In a nutshell, when writing a design you place three levels of possibilities into the design itself. The Good is the best-case scenario where everything makes it into the heart of what you want to make. The Bad is the scenario with all bells and whistles stripped out of it, leaving the core of the design idea for implementation. And the Ugly is the bare-bones implementation of the design that is just enough to fit into the game without being a hindrance to players. Adding this philosophy to your design allows for a lot of leeway down the line in the production of the game.

(And yes, project managers have cursed my name for doing this at the beginning but then celebrated me at the end.) After your design is completed and discussed, the stakeholders (code/art/production) can decide how long each level will take to implement. This aids management and production in choosing their priorities that they want the stakeholders to focus on while maintaining a schedule.

The other bonus is that if anything gets cut, or if people have more time during production than expected, another layer of any design you have built can be added as the work is already been designed out. On many occasions, I have gotten each of the groups to do estimates of time needed for every level, and that has helped me barter areas getting to a higher quality level when the schedule changes. Plus, this will make way more friends with every group and show your flexibility with change in your design. You just have to remember that if the schedule gets moved up and things need to be cut, you as a designer have to be okay with getting a boatload of your Ugly design into the game.

Steps to Success

- Write up a one-page mechanic document for a character that can run, and use the three levels of complexity ranging from having multiple multidirectional movement rates to they can just move.
- Have the next design you write be set into the three levels of complexity and present it to someone for their feedback.
- The next time you go for a coffee break, figure out the three levels of complexity you could do to obtain that coffee. This simple exercise will make you understand exactly what the three levels of complexity are.

PRE-PRODUCTION: INNOVATION VS. BOILERPLATE

The Point

Is it better to create the new or take what others have done before? It's an age-old question that has haunted most designers and should be at the forefront of your mind when creating a game.

Further Definition

Artists and designers throughout the millennia have wrestled with what people want versus what people don't know they want until you provide it. It's a dangerous concept as people naturally gravitate toward things they understand. It's safer for them than seeking out new exciting things that change their viewpoint. As a game designer, it's your job to figure this out with everything you put into a game, and from my experience you need a mix of both old and new to succeed.

Think of your product as a scale with new on one side and old on the other. Now take all your design choices for major features and assign a new or old label to each. This will give you an overview of where your game is going to be on the scale (e.g.: six new and four old equals two new on the scale). From there, do the same with the minor features set, as it can be very different. In the end, add them up together and see what you get. While this is a very simplistic view of the product, it's a good signpost to recognize the style of game you're making.

No need to think you're an innovator if all your features are reused from other products, but that might be okay too. You must remember that it's not always about breaking the mold if the title calls for a mold-heavy feature implementation. I have seen amazing products innovate some key features that raised it above its competitors even though almost everything else in the game was directly ripped from others. It's good to figure out what systems make the most sense for you to take advantage of instead of reinventing every wheel, which is time consuming for everyone as well as prone to having more errors for the player.

Now, some titles expect to be nothing but innovation that breaks any sense of a mold. Those games are the industry changers, and I'm sad to say they fail just as often as they succeed. I've seen tiny games built by one person or a small team with a unique set of features blow up in the industry. I've also seen dozens of games that were impactful to me that no one ever played, damning them to obscurity and financial ruin. It's all a matter of right features, right place, and right time. Set yourself a goal, evaluate where you are, and course-correct if needed. This means getting everyone involved early on so the whole team is on the same page with the style of game they are making. In the end, I'm sure you will find the best possible situation.

Steps to Success

- Take any game and chart out the features using the old/new scale test.
- Look up innovative games across the industry for the last year and see how they did sales-wise. Minds will be blown.
- Look up a yearly sports title and see how most use the same features year after year to succeed with very few innovations.

PRE-PRODUCTION: MAKE A MODEL

The Point

If you are stumped on how a space is going to work or it's not ready for you to design, make yourself a model. Sounds silly, but it works.

Further Definition

Models have always been a powerful tool to show people the design. They allow designers to chart multiple pathing options and set up AI placement. It's important to remember that you are not held back from your vision of the game by it not being ready for you to build. It might be a blocker in a traditional sense until all of the parts are together for you, but like many blockers in life, you can find a way around them. When one door is locked, go through the wall.

Models can be anything from placing army men on a table to spaceships hanging from the ceiling with spinning planets. The format doesn't matter, it just needs to suit you best. And it doesn't even have to be physical, as I have seen many programs out there that allow for quick environment generation to support this effort. I'm just here to remind you that any form of model can be helpful to get the level thought out.

I have seen designers work out entire games through models. They could lay out a level that allowed them to spend days going over areas like start location, pathing routes, enemy placement, item caches, big moments, and level completion. Taking some time to pore over every detail in a state that normally would have a designer blocked is a great opportunity and has allowed great design calls early in the process. Once a level is completed, it can then be documented through text and photographs to support the design—which in turn becomes the base of the written design documents for the levels. I myself have had countless hours saved because the engineering group let me know what was possible from a model proof of concept. This freed me up to focus on areas I could affect instead of designing for what would not be possible. Added to this, it also gives developers across the game a clear vision of what you as a designer are looking for. Finally, once everything is ready, having a model vastly reduces the time to implement and allows everyone to get to the testing/tuning phase much faster where the levels can be honed to perfection.

Now, I understand this doesn't work for all games, but even the very first side-scroller video games were created first on graph paper before they were implemented into the code. Models work and have helped many designers refine their concepts early.

Steps to Success

- Figure out a model medium that works best for you to plot out a level from technological to traditional. Kid's toys totally work.
- Take a level from your favorite game and plot it out in a model.
- Document the different beats of the level in text and photos to practice. Practice makes us all better. Chant this three times.

PRE-PRODUCTION: MICRO ADVENTURES

The Point

Every interaction in a game is an adventure for the player—and yes, that includes the menu systems, so treat them as an enjoyable journey.

Further Definition

I have often seen UI (User Interface) design get left out, or left until the end, and given a total lack of the love that it truly deserves. Game designers tend to leave menu systems alone as they have had little classical training in 2-D design. They want to focus on gameplay, but in many instances this is a failing that can really bring the game to a halt.

At their core most games have three menu systems that should be treated like adventures for the player to experience, instead of a tired set of menu options for them to wrestle with to get the bare basics sorted out. These are the front-end menu, which is everything before gameplay, the

HUD (heads-up display), which is the in-game menu at the peripheral of the screen, and the game menu, which is the pause menu where the player can quickly access options.

Of the three, the front end is normally the largest, as it's the player's first taste of the product. This means it needs to be an adventure that gets the player geared up for gameplay. Too many times have I been forced to watch a tiny loading animation in the corner of the screen or sit through the countless screens for companies/publishers/engines just for the honor of pressing PLAY. It's like movies and TV shows of yesteryear when they had a huge lead-up through rolling credits and monstrous intro sequences. Today these are completely gone to make room for more content to keep people connected to the media. Start to think about each journey the player must undertake on the way to gameplay and what you can do as a designer to make them better for the player. Now go and improve them.

For the HUD and the game menu, you should want to focus your efforts around quickly understandable visual language that complements the player's gameplay experience and doesn't get bogged down in complexity. Focus yourself on common iconography and bold lettering to help the player understand the world they are playing in, and always use the fewest and simplest elements needed. The game menu needs to be a resource that can be accessed and then removed to avoid breaking up the gameplay experience. This might sound like simple logic to you, but think of how many games have failed (and are still failing) at this by big game companies worldwide.

Steps to Success

- Take any game and chart its front-end adventure. Was it good?
- Select a game with a HUD you really liked and list out why it works. Understanding what is great in HUDs can be priceless.
- Look up the best game menus in games (it's a quick web search). Figure out why each of these menus is better than the carbon-copy ones we see in games too many times.

PRE-PRODUCTION: LIGHTS, CAMERA, CAMERA

The Point

In every game, the camera is its own character and window to gameplay.

Further Explanation

Most designers forget about this when planning out a game and it always comes back to haunt them, which is why I'm bringing it up here. You need to have a very defined view (yes, pun intended) for the player for all areas of your game and have that worked out in advance of any code being written. Everyone will thank you for having thought this out.

To start with, focus on the genre of the game you are creating and what types of cameras have been used in these games before you. This research shows you what has worked, what has failed, and, to be frank, what is expected in that genre. This doesn't mean it needs to be the only camera configuration, it's just the base camera that has traditionally worked. After looking into that, you will need to decide which camera works for you as the default.

Two-dimensional (2-D) cameras can be side-view (2-D viewpoint from the side only), top-down (overhead view looking down), 3/4-view (bird's-eye view, perspective slightly tilted), isometric (three-coordinate-based 2-D art at a 120-degree angle), or fake first-person (2-D blocks over pictures that give the illusion of 3-D). Most 2-D games use a single camera for their engine and build their viewpoint based on this single view.

Three-dimensional (3-D) cameras can be free (camera is completely player controlled in an environment), rotate-free (allows the camera to rotate around the player in 360 degrees), 2.5-D (2-D side-scrolling with 3-D elements), over-the-shoulder (3-D view over the shoulder of a character), center (behind or centered on the player), lock-on (focuses on a target), switch (first-person to third-person with a button press), first-person (through the eyes of the character), fixed (fixed perspective for an area or follows the character from a fixed vantage point), or free-look button (player uses a button to take control of the camera and look around). Now, unlike 2-D games, many 3-D games utilize a few cameras throughout, which means it's best to start with a primary camera for gameplay and work out the situations that could benefit from another camera's view.

The camera is our window into the game's world and can evoke emotion. Swapping to different cameras can be used for good or can be jarring. Only add cameras that add something extra—a default camera will do for gameplay.

Steps to Success

- Form a rectangle using your thumbs and forefingers. Follow a friend around with this camera frame to get ideas for camera viewpoints.
- Pick a genre of games and investigate what they use for cameras.
- Take tutorials on movie camera work. It's a good starting point.

PRE-PRODUCTION: TOOLS—LOOK TO THE FUTURE

The Point

Every artist needs their tools, whether they are external or internal. The right tools at the right time can make the difference between a crappy product going straight to the bargain bin and the triple-platinum best seller. Respect your tools and use them.

Further Explanation

At the beginning of a project, spend time getting to know your tools backward and forward to the point where you can teach them to carnival folk with five arrows in your back. If you do not have the tools you need, then make their creation an imperative to be done first.

As a designer, you need to have a large knowledge of different tools at your disposal that you can call up at any time, as many projects will utilize different sets throughout the game's production. On many a fine occasion, bugs inside a tool can be utilized in a unique manner to get mechanics into the game (one man's potato is another man's starship). If you think that mastery in just one level editor will see you through years of design, you're sadly mistaken. Spend time learning new editors on the market whenever you have a spare moment in your already busy day. If you are ever stumped on how a tool or a facet of the tool works, suck up your pride and ask someone else, as doing that saves everyone time in the long run. I cannot stress this point enough: the five minutes it takes to get schooled by someone else in how to solve a problem could literally save you hours of wasted head-banging against your computer screen.

Another key thing to remember is to evaluate your tools constantly as a best practice (a chef sharpens their knives pretty much daily, evaluating their sharpness). Create a top-ten list of improvements and bug fixes, as no tool is truly complete. You never know if a software engineer might have some spare time to hack something into your tool that will save you huge amounts of time later on. Plus, having that list sets you apart as it shows that you care enough to think into the future in case anyone ever asks for tool suggestions, which everyone respects in the long run.

Steps to Success

- Take the top three level editors on the market, get review copies, go through the tutorials, and build some levels. When done, have them reviewed by someone you don't mind hurting your feelings.
- Take the top three visual tools, get review copies, go through the tutorials, and create three distinctive works of art for each. No review needed—your art is wicked, I know already—.
- Take the top three database tools, get review copies, go through the tutorials, and create a database of erroneous data to justify you having fun this weekend with your friends. If it doesn't compute, then you don't get to play with them.

PRE-PRODUCTION: AUDIO DESIGN

The Point

Can you hear that? That's sound design. It fulfills the auditory sense needed to complete the entire entertainment experience. The band is nothing without the music.

Further Definition

Sound design, which deserves all your love and respect, typically doesn't get it even though sound is one of the five senses you live your life with. Sound design in games is the sum total of everything from the little sounds in the front-end menus to the battle-hearty orchestral tracks in gameplay, along with everything no one expects in between. Every movie you have loved has sound design in it. Every musical track you hear has a sound designer behind it even if they don't call themselves one. Sound is all around us as a species, and the moment it's removed, we feel like a limb is severed from us, as sound is one of our beloved senses.

In this period, it's best to start thinking of all the places where the sound is going to make an impact for the game and what you would like to get out of the sound experience. I say this as many game teams leave this until the very end, contract it out to audio engineers, and take what they are given when it's eventually delivered, as it isn't a huge area they care about in the grand scheme of the game. I'm here to say that those games lose out on players who feel through the audio of the game just as much as the mechanics themselves. You need to have a plan-to-goal system set out for the audio in the game.

I break up audio design into front end (menus to get to gameplay) and back end (gameplay itself). For front end, I look at what emotion I want to invoke in the player before they get into gameplay, then break out the background audio tracks along with the button interaction sounds to build to the emotion I've decided on. Break it down to build it back up again. In the back end, I break the audio into pause menus, characters, items/weapons, enemies, inanimate objects, ambient levels, ambient music, and musical tracks. This allows me to document a list of audio needed and what vein I would like it to be in. Again, this calls back to projecting an emotion to the player in the level through the sounds that you are working toward building through the smaller audio files. Added to this, you want to think about how as the difficulty gets harder in levels the audio should match that intensity to really pull the player into the game.

One of my favorite games had an ambient audio track in the levels that matched the relaxed state of a human heartbeat as I traveled through the game world. When I faced the first boss, the speed of the background music quickly increased, and I found my own heart racing to match it as I fought the boss. When I finished the boss I was out of breath solely based on the audio.

Steps to Success

- Take a game's front end and come up with an emotion for it.
- Play a level of any game without audio to learn audio's value.
- Come up with three insane improvements to an audio design.

PRE-PRODUCTION: MONETIZATION

The Point

How will your game make money? You might think you're an artist, but every artist needs to eat. Games are a business like any other.

Further Definition

Every game has or has had a price tag at one point. It costs money, time, and effort to get a game to market. This means right at the beginning you need to figure out what style of game yours will be to make its money back with enough profit to keep the company going to the next game. An ill-monetized game can destroy not just a game but a company in one fell swoop.

In today's games market, there are basically three major groups of monetization, with minor subgroups inside of them: free with purchased additions, set price, and base price with live service. These three groups make up the bulk of games on the market.

Free to play allows the player to get the game for no charge but will offer small packages, upgrades, or "pay to win faster" options. These games largely make up the mobile space. That's not to say there aren't other games in the PC/console market that might be free to play—it's just normally a mobile focus as it's been proven to work. Games of this variety depend on small microtransactions from the player to keep money flowing in.

Set-price titles can be anything from mobile titles all the way to AAA titles. The set-price model is charging the player once for the game. These can be mobile or PC/console games. They might have DLC (Downloadable Content) and additions after launch if they are successful and the company believes there is more profit to be made. This was the method for decades of games, as they normally could only provide the game on media that would fit it.

Base price with a service has a set price to buy the game but will be delivering added content over an extended period of time as a live service. This too can be mobile, PC, or console, with many games now being on all three if possible. With the advent of patch technologies it's a lot easier to add extras to a game post-launch.

There is a fine line between offering value and taking advantage of gamers, which many games companies have already figured out for you. It's a slippery slope to let greed drive your design. It's best to focus on the thought, "What would I pay for this game?" and work from there. Too many companies have bled gamers for too long, and gamers are wise to the tricks of cost. Being savvy to this situation will help you plan out the right monetization structure.

Steps to Success

- Look at the top mobile titles and how they make money.
- Look at indie titles that have a base price and how they did it.
- Look at AAA live service titles to learn what they offer.

PRE-PRODUCTION: PLATFORM OR PLATFORMS

The Point

It's important to design for a game knowing if it's going to be on one platform or many, as each has its own quirks to design for or around.

Further Definition

Games can come out on a single platform or on multiple platforms. Single platform is simple and cheap, allowing a development team to focus on fewer variables to bring the game to market. Multiple platforms are more complex to build for, more expensive, and take longer to build, but have the possibility of making way more money as the possible buying population expands. A platform with a large install base can make even a sub-par game a decent amount of profit, which means it's always worth looking at. This doesn't mean every game fits with every platform, so it's worth your time to do the research on each platform to find out what sells the best.

On many occasions, deciding the platforms might be thrust on a designer, or they might have the ability to steer the game to be on the right systems. A forced situation is usually due to a deal with that platform or production house, or perhaps the company doesn't have the funds to expand to more platforms. If you have the chance to steer a product, it's normally best to get the game on as many systems as makes sense.

The single platform lets you know its limitations, the technology it supports, and the variables you will need to manipulate to come out with the best product. Most of the time, smaller teams focus on a single platform as it cuts down the variables and with the right targeted platform allows the company to market to a specific audience without diluting the message.

Multiple platforms are the bane of most designers and software engineers, as what works for one will not work for another, creating a mountain of bugs in the game. It's like adding 3-D depth to a 2-D painting to start to comprehend what's it like building a game on multiple platforms. It's doable but very difficult. It's worth a decent amount of designer thought to come up with the right features that work across all of the platforms, as reviewers and gamers will judge the versions against each other the moment it hits the market. If the team has the time and employees to do this, it can be really profitable, as you're really building an experience with a single platform as the primary focus and the other platforms are just ports of the original experience. Most of the time, there is zero design craft put toward the platforms being ported apart from the performance and technologies meeting the primary platform. Sometimes specific platforms get features unique to them, but that is rare in today's world, with add-on items generally being the preferred differentiator.

Steps to Success

- Look into sales of a single platform game versus multiple.
- Research how the top three platforms are to develop games for.
- For one of your game ideas figure out what platform should be the primary one and if it needs secondary ones.

PRE-PRODUCTION: COMMUNICATE EARLY

The Point

COMMUNICATE! That's right, boys and girls, get off your chair and go to talk to people. Learn as much as you can naturally about everyone you are going to be working with by communicating with them.

Further Definition

I'm really not interested in your geek tendencies to hide out whenever possible as an introverted designer. You need to talk, be heard, and have the other person understand your point. I have personally seen some great designers who are locked in the silence of doom phobia that stops them truly getting ahead in their career. Don't let this happen to you, because as far as I'm concerned, designers should end up talking to more people per day than any other discipline in games.

I had the idea expressed to me once as "increasing your personal bank." The more people you communicate with, the more they will want to form a relationship, which means they will want to help you when you need it. If people use the excuse they don't have time to talk, you're not trying hard enough. You have to start using your spare time during lunches, coffee breaks, and extracurricular drinking sessions to get to know everyone you're ever going to be dealing with.

I personally had a lead engineer who wouldn't even let me into his office to talk until one evening out with friends I saw him eating alone and invited him over to share our company. After that evening of fun and entertainment, he couldn't do enough to help me with anything I needed to get sorted out, and his door was always open to me. The best part about it is that an artist or software engineer is far more likely to implement that extra bit of greatness from your design if they know you. Plus, throughout the project you will need to alter your design and that information needs to get to the right people at the right time, which means you need to know who they are. Communication errors can cause features to be cut, people to waste their time, and designers to be looked at like a bunch of buffoons. (We are not buffoons. We are better than that. We are performers for the greatest show on earth.) If you take anything away from this, it should be that your communication needs to be above reproach and without thought of any deception.

Steps to Success

- If you're introverted, start off by having conversations with strangers in elevators and have them walk away from it with a smile on their face.
- Talk to a selection of people each day that you would normally not talk to. Find out what makes them shine and let them talk about it. They will love you for it.
- Join a local speech group and take pleasure in standing up in front of people discussing any topic with perfect calm. If you're an extrovert, join a play and perform in front of a large audience.

PRE-PRODUCTION: CHARACTER GROWTH

The Point

Building in character growth is a surefire way to connect a player to the game.

Further Definition

I add this in early in the development cycle as it's something that every designer should be thinking about early on for every game. How is the main character the player is using to inhabit the game going to grow through the experience of the game? I have seen too many games where the main character is a flat archetype with a single motivation who seeks to overcome the evil that has stopped them from leading a normal life. I have saved the prince/princess too many times from the castle and I'm sure you have too if you look back on your gaming history.

I call this challenge "A to B, then Boss," which is what most games get the player to follow. Go from point A to point B in a level and then fight a boss at the end. It's simple, straightforward, and has been done to death in every game. What you need to understand first is what can be done to change the variables around the sequence of "A to B, then Boss" to help add to the player character's growth. What can you think up to change the motivations for the character, which in turn will help improve the character's arc? These external forces can help mold the player character through what they are experiencing. It's always best to chart this out, as it will give you a clear set of variables to work with. If the player character starts with a single drive, what do you want them to feel by the end of the game? Then you can lay this arc over the levels of the game to break down how you're going to get the character to that point by the end. What events need to be in the player's way to help them grow to the place you want them to end the game with? It's not an insurmountable problem to tackle, it just needs you to think in another way—break it down to build it back up again.

I myself am looking forward to the day when in a game I go questing to save a prince/princess by decree of the king/queen and along the way I learn the enemies I've destroyed are themselves fighting against a totalitarian regime forced on them by the king/queen of the land. I learn the weight of guilt and question if what I'm doing is right. Then I figure out that the prince/princess is an ungrateful blight on the people and has done unspeakable atrocities to everyone under them, forcing you to come to grips with whether saving them is the right move and, in the end, decide that they are better off in a slimy dungeon for their crimes. Which in turn leads me to start a revolution for the people, become the people's champion, and take on the king/queen in the final battle to set everyone free from the tyranny of evil. Instead of just seeing the simple and familiar story, I changed the variables, which changed the characters' motivations and brought out the characters' emotional growth. It's on you to think up how the system can be improved.

Steps to Success

- Come up with a different formula than "A to B, then Boss."
- Chart a character's growth from start to finish.
- Take a classic one-dimensional story from a game and improve it.

PRE-PRODUCTION: CONTROLS

The Point

Video games are by nature interactive, which means it's your job to figure out how a player is going to use the controls.

Further Definition

Every video game has controls and had someone do massive amounts of testing to figure out how best to perfect them so the player would have an enjoyable experience. I myself, though, have literally thrown a controller across the room when a game's controls have been frustratingly tiresome. Like many features of game design, it's a fine art of taking what others have learned and done and figuring out if you want to improve or change them for the game you're making. I've personally seen designers wrestle with the controller problem to the point where it almost drove them mad, and on other occasions I've seen designers take the best of breed from the industry to finish perfecting their controls in a week.

Often the controller itself will be forced on a designer due to the platform choice. Each platform normally has a standard controller configuration, and for each game genre there is already an expectation for how the controls will handle. I always start off by researching the best controllers I've seen or played with in the genre I'm working in. Then from there I break down all of the actions I want the player to be able to do in the world

I am designing for. I make a long list of all the possibilities I would like the player to be able to control and then cut that list down with a chainsaw to get exactly the best options that will fit on the controller itself. Remember that the controller, like a piano, has only so many options. Yet it's what we do with those options that makes music.

After I have the base configuration, I involve the software engineers and get it all hooked up. This normally happens in a test environment or gray world to see how the controls can be adjusted—many times, what works in your mind doesn't always work when it's being tested. After you have perfected the base configuration, test the living life out of it with everyone around you to figure out if it works. If you see that other additions or configurations might help the player, build them in as controller variants to help the player tweak their play experience to their own desires. The more options you offer, the better a player will connect with the game, as they can craft the controller experience that best suits them. I always make the joke with controllers that not everyone is right-handed, and that's just the beginning of the differences between one player and the next. Do your best to perfect the base version, as that will be how most players first experience the game—not everyone is like me, going into the settings first before entering gameplay to tailor the best situation for myself.

Steps to Success

- Pick up a fork and figure out all the ways you can use it.
- Research games known for horrific controls. Learn from them.
- Go into the controller settings of any game. Tweak them to learn.

PRE-PRODUCTION: DIVERSITY

The Point

Every game needs to have diversity in its design, and that means everything from enemy types to characters' ethnicity.

Further Definition

As games have evolved, so has the need to add diversity to them to encourage the player to keep playing the title. It's no good to have just one environment with just one enemy—that experience grows tiresome very quickly, and players strive to meet new experiences. They want to be surprised by the world you are creating, which presents you a design challenge.

I call this the One Crate Conundrum. The OCC is that with enough time and money infinite diversity from items to levels can be added to any game, yet designers are given a limit on both, which forces them to have to pick the best areas to focus on. You only have a limited amount of time to focus on any one area, which means that you need to set boundaries for each area you can add diversity to. This limit helps you put your entire focus on a single design area (e.g.: character skins), figure out the limit that can be achieved in the time you have and then work to achieve the goal in the allotted time. Once your goal is done you can move along to the next area in the game until all of the areas of the game have the diversity you want. It's no good to have hundreds of enemies if the player sees the same crates in every level.

If you take the OCC a step further, it's good to think how the options affect different people around the world. A certain people will look at a situation completely differently than you and jump at an item that you might perceive as mostly pointless. This diversity in thinking is based around history, education, and experience that is undoubtedly different from yours. It takes a lot of research to get into the heads of another people. The more you can do this, the better your game will be received by those people. When I was growing up, games were largely focused around Japan and the United States. Over time, countries all over the world started producing and playing games, which changes the dynamic of who you are designing for. Understanding their needs, desires, wishes, and history will arm you for creating dynamic design that will support the game being played for years to come.

Everything in a game should be a part of your scope to help get to the best it can be, and the sooner you start to realize that, the better you will be able to deliver great diverse content.

Steps to Success

- Make up a simple enemy. Set yourself a goal of ten minutes and come up with all the possible types it can be.
- Imagine a fictional fantasy game, giving yourself only ten minutes per category to come up with weapons, gear, and enemies.
- Travel the world! If that's not possible, visit a foreign or diverse area of your town.

PRE-PRODUCTION: LOCALIZATION

The Point

A game is no longer sold in just one language, which means you need to think how the language will affect your design when you're creating it.

Further Definition

Not everyone in the world speaks like you do. Hell, every country has different versions of the same language with people from different areas barely being able to understand each other when they meet. This means you need to think about each language that will be in your game and give it its just respect, because someone who speaks that language is going to play the game. I'm sure that it will be surprising for you to hear, but I have seen developers all but forget about localization until the end of a game's cycle, leaving it as cleanup work. Do you think that players in other countries got the same experience as players who speak the developer's native language? No, I thought not.

Figuring out what languages go into your game should be on your shoulders to provide to other members of your team, which takes some education about what areas or countries have the largest video game playing audiences. It's no good to translate for a country that doesn't purchase a decent amount of games, so you need to research what countries buy games of your variety. Once you have a short list, break them into primary, secondary, and tertiary locales. The primary ones (commonly English-speaking) will get 50% of your time, while the secondary ones will get 30%, which leaves 20% for the tertiary areas. This breakdown lets you give your time proportionately to each, without leaving all of them to the end with 5% if they are lucky.

Now let's break down localization. There are three levels most games use to localize titles. The simplest version of localization is simply swapping the text from the developer's native tongue to another language. This simple form turns all the written words into something digestible for another people. This is the base form of localization, but it can still help the game reach a wider international audience. The second level is to localize all the speech in the game, which is much more expensive and needs to be done by native speakers. It's not good to have a twelfth-century Japanese samurai speaking with a New York accent. Don't laugh, it's happened (well, maybe laugh a little). The third level of localization is in the game itself, where signs, markers, and items are localized for a specific people. This connects them more with the game as they can understand the world even if it's a unique one. This third level is very costly and involves the most amount of thought to bring to fruition successfully. If it is pulled off, it adds volumes to the title and can increase sales as the word of mouth plus reviewer praise in that locale can push a title into the profit stratosphere.

Steps to Success

- Watch a foreign movie with subtitles. This is the basics.
- Watch a movie that has been dubbed and see if it improves your viewing experience.
- Find a movie that specifically has scenes made for it for another locale and learn how this adds value to the people from that locale as it makes them part of the narrative.

PRE-PRODUCTION: FALLING DOWN THE RABBIT HOLE

The Point

Don't get lost in the details. It's easier said than done when you need to keep them all in your head.

Further Definition

The saying "the devil is in the details" is never truer than in game design, and it's your job to not be sucked down by them. This means you need to learn to have a healthy ability to focus on details and then move on. This simple point can be the difference between making your delivery dates and causing the project to be moved out at great expense to everyone involved. This doesn't mean you shouldn't focus on details. You just have to understand that they need rules around them to keep them in check.

Staying out of the hole happens when you set up a specific time period to achieve a goal. This nugget of wisdom comes from years of letting the details overwhelm me and spending way too much time going over minutiae that in the grand scheme of the game really didn't matter. Eventually I realized that putting goals around details is the best way to achieve success. This comes in the form of setting a solid end-result goal for the detail you're looking to achieve, steps to get there, and a timeline to get to that goal. In this way you take control of the details. Now, this doesn't mean it will always work out the way you intended, it just means you have to take steps to handle it instead of succumbing.

This breakdown and compartmentalizing of the details is not just a work skill—it's also a life skill that should be practiced, as it will help you take control of aspects of your life that might currently have control of you. Many people get sucked down with issues or details that in the bigger picture truly do not matter. It is this act of focusing and then moving on that will help you respect the details as well as allow you to carry on to better things afterward. It's hard to do, as many of us are constantly brought back to these details by others, media, and the world around us. Learning to set a boundary for them will help you overcome them. The first step is understanding that the details are controlling you, that they do not need to be, and that you can conquer any of them no matter how important they might seem when they first appear. You have to trust that you can do it and set up healthy boundaries to achieve your goals.

Steps to Success

- Take any object. Set yourself a goal to draw it, break it out into simple steps from the top of the object down to the bottom, and set a specific amount of time to complete the drawing.
- Take a feature for a game and set yourself the goal to write it up in one page. Break out the main points you want for that page and when you plan to complete it.
- Take an issue you are currently suffering with in your life, break it down to all of the variables that affect you, what you want to change about those variables, a final goal you want to get to, and a timeline to achieve that goal. Then do it. Action is rewarding.

CHAPTER 4

Production

CONTENTS

Level 4: Production 72
Production Definition 74
Production: Evaluate Each Milestone 76
Production: Ctrl-X 77
Production: Communication Catch-Up 78
Production: Maintaining the Balance 80
Production: Your Time Is Precious 81
Production: Make Villains Vibrant 82
Production: Build Parts to Combine 84
Production: Test Your Stuff 85
Production: Incentives 86
Production: Peaks and Valleys 88
Production: Visual Storytelling 89
Production: You Are Not Your Mistakes 90
Production: Spiderweb of Features 92
Production: Risk vs. Reward 93
Production: Tune It 94
Production: Difficulty 96
Production: Level Design 97
Production: What Are You Doing Right Now? 99
Production: Goal Setting 100
Production: Artificial Intelligence 101
Production: Final Feature 103
Production: The Power Is Not in Design 104

Production: Ready, Steady, Go! 106
Production: All Hail Chaos 107
Production: Keep It Stable 108
Production: Friends Make Life Better 110

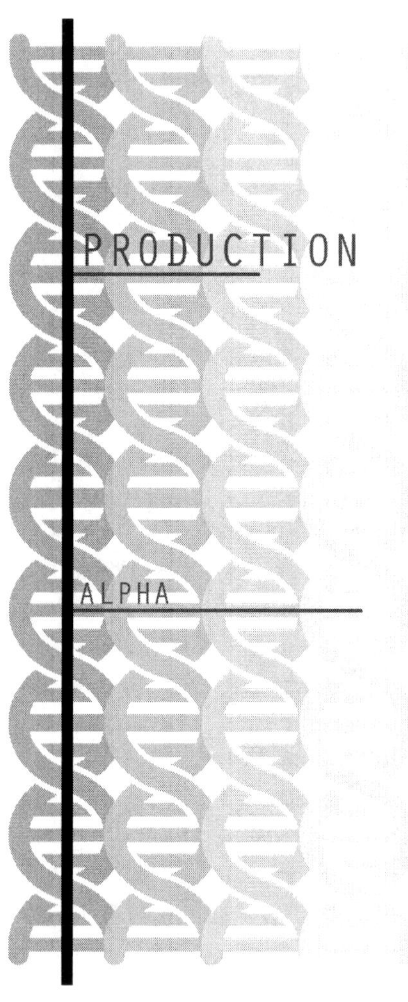

LEVEL 4: PRODUCTION

Now, I'm sure you're thinking you have already done so much, yet it's time to realize this is when you will really grind it out. This is where all the real work comes. All of the previous levels have just been there to outfit you with the skills and gear to meet this level. It's not the time to rest on your laurels, as this is the level to prove your mettle against all odds and—oh, look, another massive gate awaits you.

In your work, you will find that decisions you made in the previous levels putting all those points into certain areas now seem like boulders hindering your progression. With all of your might you will want to return to the beginning to do it right as you encounter new monsters you never accounted for. Your meticulous planning, your Blue Sky level successes are something you now just have to live with. It's on you to refuse to return to the previous levels or start it all again. It's time to forge forward with what you have.

During this level's trials, you will be asked to speed through areas, putting your all into meeting all of the minor milestones in the time that you have. They will come at you, and then out of nowhere you will have tiny periods of nothing going on, as if the mission clock is broken. You find yourself wanting to surge forward, but you will have to wait. This means you should have a bunch of side quests to keep you busy, as they will be the rescuing factor when you are without a major task. You can always be doing something.

Then, one night just like any other, you will be forced to realize that your dreams of finishing the game the way you want have to die. You're not going to get it done the way you hoped, and that hurts. Like, a lot. This will be the long, dark night of the soul where you need to fight yourself again but not in physical form, like nega you. This version is in your head and understands you on an entirely new level that seeks to rob you of your passion for the entire game. It's a difficult mission, to be sure, and something that will haunt you for every subsequent level no matter how much you pretend it hasn't affected you. If you walk out of the valley of death having conquered your inner demons, you will have more scars than you can count, but this time your allies will not be able to see them.

After a long period of meeting every milestone, meeting every date you promised, and working tirelessly, you will approach the great gate Alpha. It's a towering monument that—unlike the other gates—isn't present at first. It's a gate that looms over all the other gates for you and your allies through your actions in this level. This gate has only one doorway to get through, as a group of allies sits atop to judge your acts against the weight of quality. While they are allies who have aided you throughout the level, they exist like the two sides of a Janus coin and now must be the gatekeepers who can ban you from the next level if you've fallen short. If you don't make it the first time, there is a small window to try a few more times but with every failed attempt you see the levels ahead shrink a little. Once you make it through, you are given a tiny robot that looks like it's missing parts. Wait, wasn't this a fantasy game? Bet you didn't see the robot plot twist coming.

PRODUCTION DEFINITION

The Point

The fourth period of a games cycle is called production, where the ideas are brought into reality. Everything is created during this period, and all the hard work needs to be done before alpha is met. This is the heart of the game and where the magic is made.

Further Definition

During production, designers have both the least and the most amount of work to do, depending on assets. At the beginning, most of the workload is light because the environments, tools, features, and mechanics are not ready yet. Don't worry, there are always other things to do, which I have detailed below in this chapter. On many occasions, though, this means the designer in you has to hurry up and wait—its feast or famine. As each asset is delivered, your workload expands exponentially and often can drop onto you all at the same time, so you have to be prepared for anything.

I've personally had projects where I was forced to entertain myself for months with work around the project because there was nothing to touch, and then all of my production review arrived on the same day. To meet the milestone requirements, I spent the next 48 hours straight reviewing every asset and getting all of the groups my notes and edits to the design to make sure we stayed on course. The loss of a weekend seemed a small price to pay for helping everyone who had been consistently working for months, and it was appreciated by all, as they could continue work without missing a beat on Monday. If you take anything away from this, it's that nose to the grindstone is what you should be doing all of the time. You don't have anything to do? Then you have failed already, as you need to understand that you *always* have something to do. Perfect your design, communicate with others, learn and refine your tools … there is always work.

Steps to Success

- Learn the delicate art of hurry up and wait, as it will aid you in attacking assets when they are completed. This can be done by only allowing yourself one hour per day to play your game of choice. It's hard to learn that you must wait for enjoyment.
- Practice the skill of leaving on time when you have no work to keep you there late. Someone with proper time management is a valuable member of any team. If you have no work, LEAVE. You will be there late when it's needed, and only an idiot does it for political reasons before its needed.
- Prepare for the unexpected. I know, no one can really do this, but think about it like whatever comes up you can roll with it instead of fighting against it. Ask a friend or coworker to stop you from getting to your coffee at some point that week and try to succeed against that sudden challenge. Adventures and adversaries make us all better.

PRODUCTION: EVALUATE EACH MILESTONE

The Point

During production, the designer has many different tasks that take up their time. But no matter what happens, you must stay focused on what needs to be delivered at the next milestone, as well as looking at the big picture of every milestone that's coming up.

Further Definition

Even if your project doesn't have predetermined milestones set out by managers and production, you should be making them up in advance. This goes back to the break-it-down point I made earlier, where everything in the game should be quantifiable for you to understand along with how items might interconnect with one another. A sprinter isn't thinking about shaving a whole second off their race time—they consider the milliseconds they can cut off their time as success.

It's no good to have a character be able to shoot something if they can't move first. To use the visual again, think of the game as a pyramid that has each layer building up to the very top. Without each layer being done properly, the next layer will just fall to ruin. As a designer, you need to help chart out when everything is going to be implemented so that you can tune it when it's ready. At its heart every team—along with you, being a member of that team—will be graded on a pass/fail basis for how you reach that milestone. Failing is learning, and if it's done by any group that is a lesson for improvement, as long as work is done to actually improve upon that failure.

Even if you are not in charge of making sure the items are getting done, think about what should be finished (hypothetically) at each milestone so you can see the bigger picture of the project. As an added bonus, this skill might get you to go into other areas of the game you might not normally know existed. This is really the difference between the junior designer in the trenches getting the work done and their lead designers focusing everyone toward meeting the project's total needs. The fun part is that everyone can learn this trait—it just takes someone to actually explain it to them.

Steps to Success

- Get a project-planning program and enter in what you did throughout that week. Then spec out what you will be doing for the next week. At the end of the week, see if you held to the plan. Realize life gets in the way of even the most ironclad plan.

- At your company or school, figure out what you need to do for the day, then what you need to do for the week, and then for the month. This is the beginning of understanding how the small pieces fit into the greater whole.
- As a practice, create a fictitious web-based game and break down everything that needs to be done into point form. Move the points around into one-month blocks in a six-month production cycle, remembering everything that's needed to build out an entire game.

PRODUCTION: CTRL-X

The Point

Things get cut in games. It's a fact and a reality most people don't like to talk about, but it happens, which means you need to be ready to hit Ctrl-X at a moment's notice. Most of all, you need to be emotionally okay when a cut is made but remember to choose your battles to fight.

Further Definition

The one thing a designer never wants to hear from anyone is "We are cutting that feature" (I've cried at these words). It's a little like a doctor telling a parent, "We can save your child, but s/he's going to lose a limb." It's really very hard at first to envision the whole when it's missing that feature, but due to a menagerie of different conditions it needs to be cut to make sure the product gets out to the consumer.

It's a fine art, really, to learn to accept this pleasantly and be able to ask the question, "What are we getting in return?"—and accept that whatever the answer is you will have to live with it. On the other side, I have seen a great many times when cutting an unruly feature early can help the game in many different areas, such as leaving other features to change for the better. This leads to staff not working overtime and meeting your scheduled ship dates, which is the entire goal. To help you emotionally divest yourself, you should have a top-five cut list in your back pocket in case you are ever asked if something can get cut or downgraded. (Use Good to Bad to Ugly if needed.) You as a designer need to know what cut will cause the least damage for the most value while still making a great player experience.

You're there to turn a negative into a positive, and you need to understand that your job is to always be supplying answers instead of problems. In the same way, you need to have a list of what you as a designer would want added in if there's any available time or staff.

On one occasion, my dates were pushed out and I got to insert a Blue Sky item that hadn't occurred to anyone until the week before, which everyone had thought was crazy. We could insert it because I had it ready as a personal homework assignment.

Lastly, respond to the situation like an adult and know there are other battles to fight and better confrontations to win. You may have lost the battle, but you will win the war when the game ships.

Steps to Success

- Take one of your previous designs and decide to cut one item that, while it would be nice, does not contribute to the overall success of the game. Feel the pain.
- Take one of your previous designs you haven't touched in a while and add a new feature that will entirely change the gameplay dynamic. Feel the joy.
- Hit on a human in a bar situation whom you perceive to be way above your league and learn to handle rejection politely and with grace. Then do that again and again. You will never see these people again and should learn to not care.

PRODUCTION: COMMUNICATION CATCH-UP

The Point

It can be said that spending five minutes a day with the important people in your life will make you a better person, and that is doubly so when it comes to being a designer. You heard this already, but it's really important to stay in touch without causing people to stop working. Be stealthy and amazing—you never want to be the guy who talks more than everyone else does.

Further Explanation

As features get implemented and new items come up for evaluation, I find that the designer has to spend a little bit of extra time catching up with everyone they directly work with. Now, this is not like the casual communication mentioned before—this is much more specific and is centered on generating a much better understanding of the people you directly work with. They are your lifeline to making the project go smoothly and the game reaching its greatest potential, yet for some reason designers get wrapped up in the slog of mundane workaday functions that keep them locked to a PC for their entire shift.

This is really the time when that communication with others is essential, as it can be weeks, sometimes months, before people crawl out from their nose-to-the-grindstone mentality of creation to just talk to the others around them. Plus, when you chat with people about specific work-related areas, they tend to want to show it off and discuss how to make it better. I have personally witnessed a software engineer turn an ugly feature on the lowest level of priority into something that ended up as the shining glory of a game. Never underestimate passion in people—everyone truly wants to create greatness given the chance.

You would be amazed how five minutes a day catching up with direct coworkers about the work they are doing or what's been rattling around in their heads will give you a better perspective on what your design is doing for the game you're on. No matter what happens during this period, departments and people tend to lose touch with the entire game. It's really down to you to help keep everyone thinking positively about the end goal, as typically you're one of the few who needs to see the end result.

Steps to Success

- Spend five minutes a day talking to your team about any topic from work to media to sports. Notice how their productivity rises.
- Spend five minutes a day talking to everyone you deal with in a certain discipline (code/art/production) about project-related items. See how they begin to trust you more.
- Spend five minutes a day talking to everyone you deal with in every discipline about project-related items and what can be done to make things better. See how much they respect you. Be the positive force even when everything is a mess.

PRODUCTION: MAINTAINING THE BALANCE

The Point

Every game has some sort of balance between art, design, and code. Your job as a designer is to help them achieve as much success as possible while maintaining a balance between all three.

Further Definition

Originally this concept was brought up to me as an evaluation method for titles when I first started working in game design, and it has helped me on many occasions understand what it takes to achieve balance between them all. This method of evaluation was explained as each game or company is a mix of these three areas, and the more they are in balance, the better a title is. It's not entirely true—I have played amazing titles that over-focused on one area—but for general understanding this is a good way of evaluating games.

To visualize this balancing method, draw out a triangle (two points at the bottom and one at the top). Code is the left point (left brain being the logic side), art is the right point (right brain being the creativity side), and design is at the top (it's a mix of logic and creativity). Now take any game and list all of the positive and negative points about it in those three categories. Everything from major features to relevant art style to load times can go into this list, and the larger the data pool the better. Count up each category's positive vs. negative score (e.g.: art 15 total, 10 positive and 5 negative, which equals a total score of 66%). From here place a center point in the middle of the triangle and draw a line to each point of the percentage you have found, with 100% being the point of the triangle from the center. Now with three points for each group draw a circle connecting them all. The closer to a circle shape, the more balanced a game. In this way you can see if the game really does meet its balance between all three visually. Many unbalanced products with a low percentage score have ended up in the bargain bin and are blissfully forgotten. Don't be THAT game—do your best to balance it.

Maintaining the balance sometimes means giving up parts of a design to allow other groups to shine. At one point the game I was working on had the chance to hire two new employees and wanted to know where they could best be placed to make the game better. Each lead of the groups fought for more people, each having a list of ways that they could benefit the game. From the design side, instead of fighting I used the triangle balance evaluation with everyone, showing all the feature sets we had planned vs. the ones we wanted to add. In the end it was found that the art side was the deficient area and could best use more people to bring it up to the balance for the game. Every party left feeling heard, respected, and with a better understanding of what was needed to improve the game. I might not have gotten more features in, but the game benefited from it in the end.

Steps to Success

- Use the evaluation method on any game of your choosing.
- Use this method when putting a pitch together.
- For your next dinner out, evaluate it using the balance method with service, meal, and cost being the points.

PRODUCTION: YOUR TIME IS PRECIOUS

The Point

As we all know, being temporal beings, our life is ending one minute at a time, which means you need to learn that each minute is precious. Life ends at any moment, and the sooner you understand that, the more you will enjoy it.

Further Definition

Every designer I have met (me included) will sacrifice themselves for their first project, working insane hours for what they believe is the greater good. That's really the reason why many large companies bring in a fresh batch of newbies every project—to make sure the project gets done. Every game is made on the blood of the young unskilled, and you should respect that no matter what level you are.

After a certain period, all developers learn that staying until the wee hours, while exhilarating at first, takes an emotional and physical toll by the end. As a designer you really need to be at your best under a mountain of different situations, which means you need to rest. I didn't say sleep, I said rest. Rest is the ability to leave work at the door and focus on external pursuits that enrich your life. The sooner you can figure that out, the better a designer you will be.

If you don't have a hobby, go out and find one that calms you. If you don't think about having fun outside of work, leave right now to find that bliss. We work to live, not live to work. As much as any producer will try to convince you otherwise and possibly guilt trip you into sacrifice, you need to set your own limits on when you need to be there.

I worked with a producer who felt the weight of the project on their shoulders alone. They would wander through the office around the end of the workday, doling out extra work they told the staff needed to be done that day. This was a trap, and as soon as they left their office staff would bolt in all directions to avoid the overtime that was inevitable if they talked to them. After a while people would just say they were busy and couldn't do what was requested, which infuriated the producer. Soon enough, the producer pulled everyone into a meeting demanding everyone needed to do this work. This decimated the team morale, as they all felt forced to do the producer's bidding that meant overtime. No one spoke up, and by the end of the project everyone was burned out, loathed the producer, and when given the chance left the company at the first possible opportunity. The game was made, but no one was left at the end to do any patches or support it live, which sunk the product and the company in the long run. Learn to speak up for you and if needed for others. Learn to support everyone's work/life balance.

Steps to Success

- Leave work at the door when you leave. Even if you need to say it out loud.
- Practice overcoming obligation, guilt, or manipulation. Practice makes us all better.
- Cultivate a hobby that takes you away from work and never let that go. Your own personal growth is priceless.

PRODUCTION: MAKE VILLAINS VIBRANT

The Point

Great heroes are known as such because they fight great villains. The darkness in enemies makes the heroes shine that much brighter.

Further Definition

In many games there has been the tendency to make enemies into cardboard cutouts of what they could be just to fill in the gameplay. I've heard designers of hapless enemies who are merely present defend their choices in more ways than I care to recall, and I really have to question why. If I question why, so should you. Enemies in games from the lowest of the low to the biggest bosses could all use a bit of depth to spice up gameplay.

This problem I call "the Goblin Encounter" has haunted many a role-playing game. The Goblin Encounter is when a player character on their way to do something cooler encounters a group of low-level goblins. A small fight ensues that the player is already destined to win and they do so without issue. It's a random encounter that just fills in space while traveling to a greater adventure. These encounters are boring, tedious, and time consuming as they have little to no point in the greater narrative. The Goblin Encounter is a thought experiment to show designers that they can do better if they just put some extra thought into it.

Just like in role-playing games, video games suffer from the same issue. For years, designers have just placed enemies in an encounter to fill in the world that the art team has provided without rhyme or reason. What it takes to fix this bad habit is looking at every encounter in the game and having a reason for the enemies being present. Can that be communicated to the player through the enemies' actions, voiceover, or through the story? You have the power to make the enemies stand out with just a little intelligent tweaking.

Bosses in games suffer from the same problem. They tend to be limited to just the basest of evil intentions—the player has wandered into their territory, and they were paid to take them out. Most are a single focus of evil that the player is being asked to overcome through solving a puzzle or taking action. When done, they are just as forgettable as the enemies before them. I've found that when I ask players if they can recall a boss fight after they have played a game most only remember the ones they had trouble beating as the victories haven't made an impact. Bosses can have an impact and can be memorable with just some extra thought put into them. Why are they in that location? What is their motivation for being there? Can they have more than one motivation? The boss encounter is a closed loop where you can play with all of the variables to make it a better and more fulfilling adventure for the player to go through.

Steps to Success

- Come up with three ideas that make the Goblin Encounter better.
- Come up with three ways to improve a boss in any game.
- Take any enemy in a video game and give them a backstory.

PRODUCTION: BUILD PARTS TO COMBINE

The Point

Build a system for your design that will allow you to combine areas together easily to unlock the wonders of any game.

Further Definition

When I first started in games I shot myself in the foot by having a very limited palette to play with. My options for tuning were limited and mostly nonexistent based off the original design document I asked engineering to build for me. They returned exactly what I requested, but the moment it didn't work out or needed to be tuned it became almost impossible for everyone to manage, with any tiny change equaling hours/days/weeks of extra work. It was a right horrible mess of my own making, to say the least. Over the years I learned that it's better to ask the engineering team to build a designer a set of building blocks that can be combined in many ways instead of specifying exactly what the end result will be. In this way a designer can then use the blocks to combine them in whatever way they see fit to make rapid changes that don't inflict extra work on other team members. Plus, this unlocks creative freedom to manipulate all of the variables in ways that no one has even thought up yet to improve the game. It's a different way of designing, for sure, but one that I have found unlocks rapid prototyping, building, and tuning.

If you're wondering what I mean when I say building blocks, well, it can be anything that has a tweakable variable attached to it. Take an enemy spawn point (location trigger for enemies to appear) as an example. Instead of just having a single spawn point for one enemy triggered by the player, why not have attributes added to unlock all of the tuning possibilities? Variables like enemy spawn numbers, different enemy types, different spawn triggers, delayed spawn triggers, spawn waves options, or boss additions, just to name a few. With every spawn point like this—now a menagerie of possible choices—this allows the designer to place one spawn point to perfect through tweaking the variables (or building blocks) through trial and error without the other groups being affected. If you start to think about everything in gameplay having tweakable variables, document the ones you think will have the most benefit, and work out the variables with the engineering team early in the production phase, I know everyone will be very happy with the outcome. Plus, this allows for rapid level creation from a design perspective if there is time that can be added to the game. Just remember to keep your variables to the required ones you need as it will be extra work for the engineering team to make them all for you—you will never get everything you can think of. Just figure out the key ones that will be of benefit to you.

Steps to Success

- Take any feature and break out three added variables that will improve it as your first taste of using building blocks.
- Now take a feature and break out as many different variables you can see have merit to tune it. The more the merrier.
- Now take that list and rank them from most to least desired, with the last 20% being cut. Learn we don't always get all the toys.

PRODUCTION: TEST YOUR STUFF

The Point

You need to test everything you put into the game and evaluate it. Pretty simple thought but not always the easiest to execute. The more people play and destroy your design, the better it will be. Playtest the crap out of everything no matter what it takes. It will help you understand what is needed for the game to succeed.

Further Definition

Now, since designers are usually pretty afraid of being told their design is flawed, many don't test it out to the fullest extent that they could to make a better game. A thousand playtests will help you improve more than any other soul-humbling action. We all want to hear about how great our work is, but we seldom open the door for improvement. Failure is your friend—it leads you to greatness. As a designer, you are crafting an experience for someone you have never met, someone you spend a great portion of your time having only a limited view of.

To counter this issue, you need to conscript an army and that means everyone—and I do mean everyone. The smallest opinion can have the greatest impact. First you need to generate a battery of questions you want answered for any playtest (I'm a huge fan of the 1 to 10 rating and the "why" questionnaire). Then find every coworker, student, friend, and Joe on the street and sit them in front of your product (nondisclosure agreements might be required). After you're done, take all of the feedback and group it together, taking your top five and worst five items from the review. For your top five, figure out what could be added to make them even more spectacular. For the worst five, generate solutions with a group of designers to see what can be done to get them all into the midrange of rating. Do this repeatedly throughout the product and you will gain a better understanding of your product as well as be a proactive team member for its success. I have heard that certain companies actually base their entire project progress on reaching 10 out of 10 by weekly playtesting and fixing everything that is wrong for the next week's test until that goal is reached. The mythical 10 out of 10 is the Shangri-La of games and should be a goal you are focusing on even if it's not achievable with the project's timeline. The point is to try.

Steps to Success

- Start off small with a core group of people from every discipline in your company, school, or friend group and give them a simple 20-question survey.
- Next, increase that group by ten more random people and repeat the experiment (yes, this is an experiment).
- Finally, graduate to a mass group of strangers you have never seen before and repeat the experiment, gathering all of your historical data into a finely tuned evaluation report … then DO SOMETHING ABOUT IT!

PRODUCTION: INCENTIVES

The Point

Every game needs incentives to drive the player to do what you want them to. Without them players would wander aimlessly, grow weary without knowing what to do, and turn off the game.

Further Explanation

Why did you get up today? Was there an incentive to leaving your bed, to going to work, to making friends, to starting or maintaining relationships, to succeeding at a vocation? Life is made up of incentives to keep us as people focused around goals. If I can make it to X, then I will be happy and so on. In any game there is the need to create incentives for the player to keep them attached to the experience. It's easier than you would think to come up with incentives as many players run toward goals before they understand them psychologically. Games have trained people to search out a goal before they even understand the game.

The harder part is narrowing the incentives for the game into a few groups of top-notch incentives. As with many elements in design, it's about breaking it down to build it back up again. This means first come up with the grand point or goal for the player. This is the nucleus of the game and sits at the center of all of the other incentives. From there, like a word bubble chart, build out the next set of major incentives that come from each level/experience. These incentives help build to the nucleus but can be quite diverse at the same time. After that, add the smaller to smallest incentives that exist in every level to get players to just go in the direction you want them to go. Once you break all of them down, make sure they are equally spread throughout the levels (no one likes an uneven incentive experience), and build back up to the larger incentives that call directly to the nucleus of the goal, you will have a plan. Now stick to and execute it.

Don't forget Easter eggs as incentives as well, as they have become a special experience many fine designers have added to a game. These little incentives are unique to the game and the designer, from the original one that just had the designer's name to unlocking another entire part of a game to experience outside of the regular play space. The Easter egg is a place to unlock your own imagination and come up with something great. Most Easter eggs now have grown in complexity, which means you will need to get your team involved to help build out something extraordinary. Have a good pitch for your Easter egg that excites your fellow developers, as Easter eggs are often built outside of regular work hours through the passion of a few.

I heard of a group of games created in Russia during the Cold War that had no incentives. I was flabbergasted as to how this could be done, and then I realized they were created in the logic of communism, where there are no winners and losers. The game was just an experience that the player enjoyed for a period. Not all people have the same goals.

Steps to Success

- Create a nucleus incentive of a game you want to build.
- Create ten incentives for your game that will help drive the player.
- Come up with an outrageous Easter egg for a game.

PRODUCTION: PEAKS AND VALLEYS

The Point

There will always be periods in the development cycle when you will have nothing to do and periods when you have way too much to do without enough time to get things done properly. Understanding that these periods are a fact of game development life will help you conquer both.

Further Definition

No one ever tells you that there are times when there will be no work. It can be days or weeks, yet every hour feels like an eternity. A traditional workplace job has you clock in, work on what you can, and clock out at the end of the day. Sometimes in game design you can be put on hold just like the pause button on any game. This is normally because the game is totally broken until the team fixes it. This is a reality of working on code that's a work in progress.

When you need to wait you need other work to keep you busy. As the game is broken, you are cut off from affecting the game directly, leaving you really two choices: "in" or "out" of the game.

"In" the game may not necessarily be in the game itself, as the build is broken, but has more to do with mindset and priority. The mindset of "in" has to do with affecting changes without viewing them. This can be in the form of making changes on a local build that might still be stable, making alterations with a level editor that can be checked in later, or focusing on supporting others in pursuits that keep you inside the game. You might think this is the only answer, but that's not always true—there might be priorities outside of the game that need your attention if the game is borked.

"Out" is the mindset of fulfilling the needs outside of the product itself either for your position or on a personal basis. For the position this can be a great opportunity to update your documentation (everyone always needs clean documentation), working on areas outside the game like better process or helping improve the team's health are worthy of your time. The other side of "out" is just that—go out of the work space to keep yourself on an even keel. This can take the form of reading a book, doing research on a topic you haven't had the time to focus on, or finding a way to relax. One of the best examples of a good "out" was a designer I worked with who had worked a heap of overtime. On the day the build broke, he told us to give him a call when it was back up again—he would be in the café around the corner, where he sat, drank coffee, and sketched. He came back in far better spirits than those who just sat around waiting.

Steps to Success

- If your game is broken, find three "in" tasks you could do
- If you game is broken, find three "out" tasks you could do
- Learn that this happens and the best you can do is to stay busy.

PRODUCTION: VISUAL STORYTELLING

The Point

Games are no longer just text-based adventures, which means that the visuals take on a life of their own. They need to have a part in the story, not just be background noise.

Further Explanation

Now, not to besmirch text-based adventures in any way—I have played some in the last few years with extreme enjoyment—it's just that 99% of games now have a visual element to them. Most developers think of the art in a game based on their own sense of artistic style, which equates to "I like it" or "I don't like it." Instead of this binary way of thinking, designers in concert with the art group can work out ways to enrich the game through the visuals. I call this visual storytelling, as it treats the art in the game as another character that evolves through the gameplay experience.

Visual storytelling is about setting up an experience from a visual standpoint to lead the player naturally through a level. This can be as easy as putting a light at the end of a hallway to something as complex as building a maze for the player to traverse. This little bit of extra thought put into the visuals is something I've seen left out rather than focused on in many games, when developers were more interested in completing the work than in making the work shine. In the few games that have done this right I have found myself marveling at the thought put in.

Coupled with this, it's always good to add symbols into your visual storytelling. Symbols themselves are very powerful and have been used by humans for centuries to explain complex ideas in a minimal visual language. Now, symbology is a tricky thing and can sometimes backfire on a designer, as a symbol's meaning to one set of people in the world can mean something completely different to another in a different location. Focusing on symbology from the core locals where you're planning on selling the game is the best bet to achieve success.

I once saw a designer testing out a level constantly feeling like he was failing, as all the testers kept going in a different direction than the designer had intended. After lamenting about this to one of the artists on the team, the artist said they had a solution. The artist made the change and they all ran the test again. When the testers got to the intersection this time, the intended door had an Exit sign above it and without a moment's thought the entire test group automatically went through it. One visual element saved the entire pathing problem.

Steps to Success

- Research visually stunning games that use visual storytelling.
- Research common symbols of the locals where you want to sell the game.
- Select a goal such as going to a local shop. Now plot out the adventure as if you have never gone before, like levels of a game. In each of these levels, what visual elements could you add to help get you to the goal at the end?

PRODUCTION: YOU ARE NOT YOUR MISTAKES

The Point

I can say this until I'm blue in the face, but you are not your mistakes, you are your achievements. The problem is you must believe it.

Further Definition

Mistakes in a game design position routinely come in two forms: personal and professional. Both of which are nasty and will do their very best to dethrone you from whatever throne you have built for yourself. On your best of days you're susceptible to each, and no amount of planning will help you deal with them. This section is not about avoiding mistakes but coming to grips with them to learn more.

On the professional side, you will make mistakes in documentation, design concept, implementation, and execution. What you thought looked great on paper in one of your designs might be the worst experience when fully implemented. When this happens, I'm here to say it's your job to take that cutting wound and be better because of it. Own up to it, speak your apologies out loud, and admit freely that it did not work out. Easier said than done when your ego is involved, but it's important to let others know you are human. After this admission you need to follow up with what you're going to do to remedy the mistake. As everyone has failed, it will elicit understanding and a drive to help you out of it. Just remember to always come with your hat in hand and check your ego at the door.

Personal mistakes take the form of communication mistakes in the categories of text conversations, emails, and verbal exchanges. I myself have made a huge amount of verbal mistakes with others or let my emotions overwhelm me. That means you get to learn from my mistakes and be better by understanding that people are not out to attack you when they disagree with you. If you have fallen into this trap through miscommunication, it's important to try to emotionally distance yourself from the conversation. Take a deep breath, center yourself, and respond in a positive manner. If you find yourself in a situation where you can't make this happen, I suggest separating yourself from the entire thing. Some distance will allow both parties to think on what they have said, come to grips better with what they are looking to achieve, and calm down all the impulses that are forcing them to miscommunicate.

Whether personally or professionally, you're going to make mistakes. Be kind to yourself, and be kind to others—you really don't know what they are going through. Accept your scars from mistakes and remember them, just don't let them drive you.

Steps to Success

- Think of your last mistake at work or home. How did you handle it?
- The next time you make a mistake, own up to it immediately and have a solution for it.
- Forgive yourself. Think of a mistake you are still carrying. Stop and let it go. It doesn't need to live in you anymore rent free.

PRODUCTION: SPIDERWEB OF FEATURES

The Point

As all the features start to come online, suddenly all of them start competing against each other, and you need to sort out how they all work together.

Further Definition

When first designing out features and how they interconnect with each other on paper, it can be easy to see all of the features working harmoniously together. I myself have thought that everything working in a design document meant that it would work when finally implemented. Well, I'm here to say that no matter how much you put down on paper, features will do their very best to fight with one another like squabbling siblings. Funny as that sounds, it's the plain truth. Many features meant to work with/around each other usually don't. They don't have all of the bugs worked out of them or haven't been fully fleshed out. This means you have to learn to balance them against each other as early as possible. On many simple indie games, this can be very easy as there are fewer variables, but as the product complexity grows, the interconnected feature web also grows.

I always think of it visually as a spiderweb with you and the game at the center as the spider. With each circle around the spider connected to the ground lines you have a feature. You're there to make sure the web is being crafted properly. As more features are added, the circles around the spider grow, and in the end what was originally supposed to be a simple design has turned into a massive interconnected masterpiece or debacle (depending on how you look at it). When there is a problem with one of the circles, you have to rush over to fix it, making sure to keep the integrity of the web together. As the development of the game continues with new features added, all manner of things fight against the web to destroy it. This means you need to always feel what the web needs and be there to fix the issues.

When you think the features are not working well together, see where the features' interconnected points lie. Next, like many areas of design, break down where the areas affect each other, stripping down the features to their bare bones. I've found many a time that if I strip the feature down it works very well with the other features, which then allows me to see how adding to the complexity helps fix any issues between them. You just have to be prepared for letting go of areas you thought you wouldn't need to revisit again. It might feel counterintuitive at the time, like three steps backward for one step forward, but if it helps you get to the end of the course, then it will have been all worthwhile instead of hobbling you for the entire ordeal. There is no shame in cutting something that didn't see its full potential instead dragging the entire game down. Just learn when it's needed and cut once early instead of many cuts later.

Steps to Success

- Go find a spiderweb as it will visually help you understand interconnected features.
- Take any bad movie in a franchise, work out all the issues and how they could be improved for the viewer to get a better experience to improve the franchise.
- Find an object you own and don't use. Let it go.

PRODUCTION: RISK VS. REWARD

The Point

Every game has a sense of risk to achieve a reward. It's the carrot at the end of the stick that the game is making players chase after. But is the carrot worth it?

Further Definition

Fundamentally, players play games to get the reward of playing and completing a game. It's a very fixed relationship where the game sets out the rules and the player abides by them until the game is completed. This works when the game presents the risks properly for the rewards the player will come away with.

Throughout the entire game it's expected by the player that a game starts off easy and grows to extraordinarily difficult by the end, thus creating a scale of challenge that naturally arcs upward across the entire play experience. Along the way it's also expected that the rewards for overcoming those difficulties will be worth it to the player to keep going. It's no good to make a player slog through dozens of levels and then offer them a weapon that is barely better than the one they have been fighting with. Situations like this cause the player huge amounts of consternation and end up with the title being tossed if it happens too many times. As a designer it's your job to figure out the system to support the added risks by offering the appropriate rewards.

To understand the optimum difficulty arc, think of a 90-degree right angle with a line at the 45 degree going outward. This 45-degree angle starts at the corner, the zero point or beginning of the game, and as gameplay levels are completed the arc of difficulty should go up to match this angle. This means you will need to work out the easy/hard difficulty for every level and map that to the right angle. This will give you a range to work from or to keep your game in. You want a flow of risk that is acceptable for the player. I call this the Player-Designer Covenant (PDC) which states that I as a designer will not screw over the player, and the player will keep playing the game until completion. If I break this covenant, then I fully expect the player to do the same.

Once you have the difficulty arc, it's rather easy to figure out the rewards for the player. Using the same right-angle chart you have for difficulty, map the best selection of rewards for the player as the gameplay experience comes to fruition. In this way, you can break up each of the rewards the player will get and lay them out across the entire product for tuning. It's no good to give the player the best item in the first level as they will not want any other for the entire game. It's good to start them off slow and sprinkle the rewards over the levels to make sure the player is getting their proper due.

Steps to Success

- Go ask someone you find attractive out. No risk, no reward.
- Make your own right-angle chart and build out a reward system.
- Now use this chart for a daily quest in your life. Did it fulfill the PD C or fail it?

PRODUCTION: TUNE IT

The Point

Whenever some new feature comes online, jump to it as fast as possible. One of the most important points for a designer during the production period is tuning the product to make sure it's a seamless experience for the end user.

Further Explanation

That means countless hours spent evaluating everything you have designed with a critical eye for quality. That doesn't mean to say you should remake the wheel, but little additions and subtractions from the first implementation of the feature are really what helps the game play at its greatest potential. If you have the gall to remake the wheel from scratch when you are reviewing it, you have already failed, so learn to work with what you have or get production to cut the area early. Harsh statement, I know, but nothing is quite as shoddy as a designer who remakes a feature after they have seen it put into the game. It's called a total lack of vision and communication, and designers who do this should be punished.

When reviewing, grade every new feature from 1 to 10, and list your top-three best points and your worst three points. Next, sit down with the person or people who implemented it to ask for their feedback on it. Generate a list of fixes from these two evaluations and send them to the employees who implemented it to fix. After that, spend a little time away from that feature and give it some decent thought now that you have seen your written design turned into actual pixels. When I was a junior designer, I had a bad habit of returning feedback that day until my lead forced me to go home and think about it before I sent it in. Believe me when I say it improved my design tenfold by just separating me from it.

After the fixes are completed, review it all over again. Every feature should get at least three review tuning sessions per project—more if you have the time. The more an artisan reviews and refines their work, the finer the end result will be. Just remember, your changes have an effect and can cause many other people to work countless hours for your opinion, which means you really need to have all of your ducks in a row before offering anything up for changes. Have a thought behind the thinker you can easily explain to support any of your tuning changes. After years, I now try my best to get the design to 80% on implementation and tune the last 20% until it's solid for launch. It doesn't always work out that way, but it's a good target to strive toward.

Steps to Success

- View the new feature for tuning with a critical eye from an end-user perspective (harder said than done, I know). Play it like a player would.

(Continued)

- Work with and communicate the great and terrible things about the feature to the people who implemented it, collecting their thoughts on it.
- Learn to look at a screen for more hours than you can imagine, because no matter what feature it is there will always be more features coming.

PRODUCTION: DIFFICULTY

The Point

Tuning the difficulty of the game is just as important as gameplay itself. If you mess it up, no one will finish your game.

Further Definition

For years I've treated difficulty as its own character in a game that I am trying to perfect and who directly fights against me at every possible moment. To understand a game's difficulty, you need to learn there are three major sets. One is the surface level which arbitrarily sets the difficulty across the entire game, the second is the difficulty ramp throughout the game itself, and the third is the difficulty inside the levels themselves.

The surface level of difficulty is normally set at three levels—easy, medium, and hard—and is defaulted to medium for the player. A few games break with this set convention, adding in layers above hard with crazy names like "'Inferno" or "Insanity" to scare the player. Those are meant for the ultra-hardcore player, but it's always best to create the game with what you would consider medium. From there you can work with the engineering team to strip back enemies and trials for the easy difficulty or add enemies and trials for hard. It sounds simple—and it really is! Most overarching difficulty areas are set like this without the player knowing about it. It's an under-the-hood feature that most players think has way more fine-tuning put into it, but it's just about setting limits to the game through the code, which you can then tune to make it work.

It's best to break up the difficulty ramp throughout the gameplay by the levels. As an example, if you have ten levels, make a chart with difficulty vertically from 1 to 10 and the levels horizontally from 1 to 10. Then create a curve arcing up to the highest difficulty level. This will show you what each of the levels should be like difficulty-wise. From there you can get a sense of the obstacles you need to pit against the player for them to finish the game. Now, if you're asking why it's a curve and not a line, well, it's been proven that players need some time to get used to a play style before the onslaught happens. The curve helps them naturally start easy to gain experience for the first few levels before the challenges really hit. No matter what, though, avoid ramping the difficulty too fast, as that will just piss players off.

The final difficulty rung on the ladder is the individual levels themselves, which you can tune to find out what makes the most sense. With the chart I explained above, you can figure out with each level how to craft a challenging experience. You can use the same curve for each level, but that doesn't always work with the story. It's smarter to set a difficulty across the level itself that makes the most sense and services the great difficulty arc you have decided on.

Steps to Success

- Play a game with each level of difficulty to learn more.
- Chart a game's difficulty level you have played.
- Chart three levels you have played in a game's difficulty.

PRODUCTION: LEVEL DESIGN

The Point

Level design is the minutia of the gameplay experience from beat to beat and makes up the gameplay experience every player enjoys.

Further Definition

Level design is a blanket term for design that deals directly with the environments of a game for the creation of levels, stages, and/or missions. Levels are the smaller experiences that build up in total to the entire experience of the game itself. Each has a personality of its own and—if you have done your job right—has a feeling that the player is left with when they complete it. Knowing how to build your own levels and script a situation into them is massively important knowledge for all games.

If you want to understand level design better, think of it having a beginning, middle and an end. This compartmentalizes it into sections that can be designed for. Then from here you can figure out the story you want each level to tell. No two levels should be the same—that will bore the player to death, which is always something you're trying to avoid. Inside each of these levels, you can then break it down further into encounters the player will experience. Inside of these encounters, the designer can take all the elements of that situation and work at perfecting them against what they want to have for the entire level.

I like to think of each level as my own personal musical compilation (or mix tape, for the old-schooler) with highs and lows that create a story I want to tell. This auditory example lets me think of music for each encounter and in turn a template that tracks mood onto the encounters themselves. In the end, I should have a well-put-together album that is a feast for the player to enjoy, which will be the level design. Just remember to add diversity to the level itself like musical tracks in the compilation.

You should get to basic level designing as soon as you have a world to build in. It doesn't matter if the art hasn't been added—you should be able to create from the moment the level is presented. I mention this because level design and perfection take a large amount of development time. You just need to find the right level of implementation that works for you. Some designers like to put in everything and then tweak from there, which, while time consuming, can lead to just small tweaks at the end. Others prefer to quickly implement only the basics needed for the level and then tweak it all through playtesting. Each designer is different, and realizing the best way for you to work with this early on will help you better communicate your intentions to the team around you. No matter what, give the level design its due respect.

Steps to Success

- Take a level in any game and break it down into its parts to understand this better
- Make your own mix-tape level compilation using music you love.
- Figure out if you are an all-up-front or bit-by-bit designer.

PRODUCTION: WHAT ARE YOU DOING RIGHT NOW?

The Point

Seriously, what are you doing right now to make the game better? If that's not your mantra, then get out of the design trade.

Further Explanation

So you have been slogging away in the pits of development on features, mechanics, bugs, meetings, and answering email (there is so much email). All this fills up your day past capacity. When during all of this heavy work was the last time you asked yourself, "What am I doing right now to make the game better?" Been too long, huh? And no, all of that stuff I mentioned above doesn't count, because that's what every common developer does as routine to get the game made. The basics are just pedestrian. You're a designer, which means you have to kick it up a notch every chance you have and make the game better wherever you can see it.

Figure out where the game needs some love and focus an extra 20% of your already 100% packed day. This is how you turn a mid-ranked game into an award-winning triple-platinum seller. You can't stop asking this question, as this is not just a one-off or systematic check that can be set up to update you. This should be in your head in your quietest of moments.

Then, when you have figured out what you can do to make the game better, YOU NEED TO GO AND DO IT! I don't care who you have to talk to, sell snake oil to, or romance over a candlelight dinner to get it done, you're there to get the finest product on the market in spite of everyone else who lacks this understanding. I've seen so many people just put in what they think they should for a project and when it fails they can't understand why it failed. Yet when they ask other developers, each one has a laundry list of possible improvements that could have been added. No one ever thought to do something about it because they were too busy doing what they thought their job was. You should be there to remind everyone that putting in that little more can unlock huge success.

I used to randomly poll my designers at the most inappropriate moments about what they could think of right then to make the game better, always expecting an answer in the time it took to blink. I'm sure they loathed me for constantly putting them on the spot, but hey, I just hope that through repetition I got it into their heads that they could always improve the game—and that's exactly what I am doing for you now. Only through repetition, perseverance, and getting out of your comfort zone can you learn to better yourself as well as the game.

Steps to Success

- Learn to ask the question at least three times a month.
- Learn to ask the question three times a week and then do one of the answers.
- Learn to ask the question daily and do everything that pops into your head for the betterment of the game. If you're truly hardcore, you don't get to go to the bathroom unless you come up with a new advancement.

PRODUCTION: GOAL SETTING

The Point

In games as in life, it's good to set goals. Goals set out a course, how you're going to get there, and what you wish to accomplish.

Further Explanation

Setting yourself goals to complete is one of the most basic precepts of design. But you would be amazed how often, as time and complexity creep in, designers leave loose threads uncompleted while they polish other areas. Worst of all, these unfinished threads make it into the released product and sometimes are the only things that reviewers or players focus on. I've seen many a fine game get 97% right across the board but make a stupid mistake that tarnished the entire experience. When the producers and designers are asked how the mistake made it in, they come up with a menagerie of excuses that really boil down to they didn't make that flaw a priority. They just thought it would be overlooked or that they could get away with it.

This is a reminder that setting yourself goals—for areas, features, levels, *anything*—is in your best interest. See it through and make sure that the entire product is solid. Having a clear view of the goal you want to get to allows you to break down how you're going to get to it, working your way backward to the moment you are in now. I added this section in as I think it's really important to start setting goals in the production period. This is when almost everything comes in from other development disciplines, which stretches your time. Stretched time pushes out the ability to get the features tuned as you're chasing the next development milestone. I've found that the sacred art of the sticky note allows me to keep present all of the goals I set. I litter my workspace with them as visual reminders that I will not rest until they have all been accomplished. I even add in steps to the goal as other sticky notes chained to the goal. Once I have completed them, I put them into a file I keep for each project to remind myself what goals I accomplished.

Well, now that I have filled your head with all that positive goal setting for the game to progress, I also need to warn you about the dangers of unattainable goals. Learn to set yourself goals you know can be accomplished. I have seen designers make wild goals about remaking features that never come to fruition. This is a waste of time for the designers, the development team, and the game itself. You have a limited time to complete the development of the game, so act accordingly with goal setting for the time you have. Start small—a goal a week is a good place to start when you're new and allows you to scale accordingly with experience. No matter what you set as a goal, though, you have to do it. Get it done.

Steps to Success

- Set yourself a goal to create three game features in any genre.
- Finish the goal.
- Set yourself daily personal goals to learn to do it for the game's sake. The more you practice this in life, the better the game will be for it in the long run.

PRODUCTION: ARTIFICIAL INTELLIGENCE

The Point

Artificial intelligence or AI is the governing logic for machines that are programmed to "think" like a human and mimic the way a person acts.

Further Explanation

AI design is a very complicated and often underrated area of game design. It shouldn't be, but the old axiom applies here that if there is nothing to complain about, then the job was done right, which leaves the AI designer in the background. Many times a software engineer will work with a designer to come up with the best possible AI for each situation, breaking them up into groups to assign different goals, to which are affixed any AI type in the game.

To understand the basics of AI design, start with a goal. Every AI has a primary goal that they are going to try and follow against all of the variables set against it. Once the primary goal is set, the designer can start to add in all of the variables that might affect the AI on its way to accomplishing its goal. If there is a curb with the goal on the other side, then the AI will need to be able to traverse the curb. I really find AI design fascinating. It's a complex set of directives governing a set of behaviors that I find myself always wanting to mess with. I want to add more variables whenever given the chance to make the AI something that the player will accept more readily as real instead of outright rejecting as a game puppet. A good AI can make or break any level, which means the more time you get to perfect it, the better the gameplay will be.

To explain this in more detail, I present the concept of "the Guard Riddle." This is a creative challenge to come up with the most human guard AI protecting a gate. I've posed this as homework to many different designers to make a set of goals for the AI to be the best guard possible, and they have come back with many great behaviors to maintain the goal of guarding the gate. One time a designer brought up a set of directives that blew me away. His premise was to have the guard faking being asleep to lure in the players. It was simple, different, and very human. As a test, we tried it out on a game we were developing. We created an openable gate, an alarm, a consequence for the alarm (or trap), and added all of the AI directives to the guard. We set another designer to open the door. The designer fell for the whole plot, but instead of being impressed, he was angry. He felt duped, as he visually expected that the AI was sleeping and that with stealth he could open the door. We tweaked the behavior and tried it out the next day. His change was that he had the AI pretending to be asleep occasionally open one eye, and if the player got caught, the guard would exclaim, "ah-ha, I fooled you!" It worked for the playtest and they both agreed the guard had achieved its goals. This is one of many solutions to the riddle.

Steps to Success

- Create an AI with a simple goal directive.
- Now put that AI in an environment and add variables to overcome.
- Create a solution for the Guard Riddle. What is the most creative solution you can come up with to solve the problem?

PRODUCTION: FINAL FEATURE

The Point

Completing a full feature with all the bugs closed in production is the best way to guarantee a stable alpha and reduce your bugs downstream in development.

Further Definition

Many game developers try to build all of the parts and pieces during development in a sprint to get to the alpha period, where they then switch gears to fix all of the features' bugs that they pushed aside to get to the milestone. This has been the classic method of dealing with games development for years, but that doesn't mean it's the best way to do it.

From experience I can tell you that building an entire feature from top to bottom in the production period is an advanced way to get fully articulated sections into the game early, which gives you all the time needed to tune them. Not only does this benefit the designer, it also helps anyone adding to the game as the feature is completed and available to work on. This early implementation allows the feature to be shown off for milestone demos and does a lot for team morale to see finished work in the main version of the game early.

To do this, the feature will need to be broken down into sections or phases for each group to work through. The engineering group begins putting the feature together with the designers. Once the base implementation is complete (this is phase 1), it's handed off to the QA group to go over (phase 2), who return bugs around the specific feature. QA then works with the developers to fix the bugs that everyone decides need to be closed (phase 3) for the feature to be final. This allows teams to shut down areas of the game sequentially instead of finishing half the features before alpha and the other half after alpha.

The downside to this method of development is that it's much harder to project-plan for, because it's next to impossible to figure out how long the bugs found on the feature will take to be fixed. This is primarily why producers and project managers like the traditional style of development as it's something they can properly control. This doesn't mean to say that it cannot be done, it just requires an inventive project manager—and those are normally few and far between. I've seen it done and been a part of it to great success, which is why I raise it up here as a possibility.

Steps to Success

- Draw half a picture only using the left-hand side of the paper. Now put it aside for a week. Come back to it to finish the right half. Doesn't that feel weird as a creative process?
- Look into different ways of developing games. You might find one that is better for you or your group.
- Try a different development method from your normal one to test out if it improves your output. You never know unless you try.

PRODUCTION: THE POWER IS NOT IN DESIGN

The Point

The true power of a game team is not in design, and you will have to get over that fact really fast. Every team has a primary area that makes more of an effect on the others, and it's very rarely in design. You need to figure out where that power is.

Further Definition

Now, I'm sure you're thinking, wow, this sounds like more stuff than I can handle and requires so much control to get the game finished to your standards. Well, there is a fine line you have to dance, because design is not where the power lies in the game team, to many people's shock.

Typically the power lies with production. If designers had their way, a game would never come out, because we would still be adding new features every moment possible and refining them until the end of time itself. The production team is there to make sure that the game meets its dates at the highest quality level it can within the time it's been given. This means you don't have the power to get everything you want in or everything you want done. It will make you have to think smarter, not harder about how to make sure you're satisfied with the end result. On the flip side, if used properly design has way more room to get things done because the leader has conventions that antihero designers do not need to follow.

I found a production team once that was taking a boatload of feedback from the games forums and using that as items they wanted augmented and improved in the game. Instead of blindly following the masses, I thought it better to use the situation to my advantage by planting contentious items that I wanted dealt with first. This was done by a trusted forum user who then drummed up pages upon pages of discussion, catching the producer's eye. Needless to say, the next week my top ten items I wanted dealt with were sent out by the production team without any of them being any the wiser. Remember, you are not the king in the castle, you're his trusted magician who helps focus the populace views to get the job done—even if you sometimes have to use the dark side to your advantage.

Steps to Success

- Whatever you do, avoid making enemies in a development team. You are not the king, and you can get stabbed in the back by anyone. Genuine friends will take a dagger for you, which is good to learn.
- If a production member makes a decision you don't agree with, request a chat with them privately to discuss the pros and cons, as a public debate doesn't always help. Do this sparingly to show you're questioning the right things. Win battles, not wars.
- Only the gods of design bestow king status on designers, and it seems that they currently number in the range of my ten fingers. Out of millions of developers, that's pretty low, so get used to being a magician.

PRODUCTION: READY, STEADY, GO!

The Point

It's important to learn your own creative rhythms when it comes to design and when you're at your best to charge over that open minefield.

Further Definition

Everyone is different, and yet everyone is typically put into a daily cycle that is meant to suit the general population instead of garnering the best possible creativity out of people. People wake up, they go to work, they work, they come home, they rest, they sleep, repeat ad nauseam. These systems of order are put in place for the general populace around the world with small variations dependent on country. This doesn't mean, though, that you're creative or any good at your job within these cycles, and you need to figure that out.

Now, I'm sure you're asking, well, how am I supposed to figure out when I'm creative? It's no easy feat and takes a lot of mistakes. First off, it's good to map out for yourself all of your periods of being creative, logical, introspective, and social. Every day is a combination of these periods, and most of us move through them by nature, having perfected balancing them in our daily lives already, but we have neglected documenting it. With a daily chart you can start to see which time periods you have naturally gravitated to for creativity. When I first did this, I found I have small periods throughout the day that allow me to be creative, but when it comes to being the *most* creative, the trend was that evenings from six to midnight are my most creative times each day (that's when I wrote this book). I suggest charting your experience and testing out different variations each week to see what works best for you. Once this is in place, I can assure you your output will increase as you're taking advantage of you being at your best.

I know a great many wonderful people whose creativity best sparks for them in the hours away from work and who have found entertaining ways to bring their genius to their professions. I once worked with a brilliant level designer who could not for the life of him wake up in the mornings—typically he came in at 11 a.m. every day, checked his emails, organized his workload, and then went for lunch at noon. At one in the afternoon he would start working and plow through work at an amazing pace. Around seven he would go home for dinner and then go back to working until one in the morning. This was how he was best creative and when the best work would come out of him. Instead of fighting about it with the company he worked for, he just organized these periods as working hours—and the company was more than willing to oblige because his output was staggering in comparison to a regular workday. He shaped what worked best for him, and you can do the same if you know when that is on a regular basis.

Steps to Success

- Chart your creative, logical, introspective, and social periods each day for a week.
- Figure out the best times for you to be creative and use them.
- Test out different periods to find the one that works best for you.

PRODUCTION: ALL HAIL CHAOS

The Point

It will happen on every project that at one point all of the careful planning, colorful graphs about productivity, and thoughtful meetings get thrown right out the door in front of an oncoming bus that doesn't even think about stopping as it plows into a building toppling it into a crater of destruction. That's chaos, and that's totally natural.

Further Definition

In the words of a great writer, DON'T PANIC! At a certain point in the production of any game, chaos takes hold and rough seas are all you can see until your ship is safely in port. Personally, this is my favorite time, and it truly does last until the end of the project where sage decisions by the right people are the only things that keep the game from the trash bin. It's also important to remember that making the right choice in chaos is a pass or fail situation with little to no margin for failure. You need to think what will fix the issue or bug as fast as possible with the least amount of knock-on issues even if that means augmenting your design. I have seen great producers and designers crumble when they no longer have the control they have relied on to keep their sanity going around a project. Instead I take a comment from my favorite senior producer I've ever worked with as doctrine: "The real trick is to absolutely give up your control to chaos and learn to surf the waves instead of fighting against them." The best any of us can hope for is to see a problem, dive deep into it, sort it out, and then go back to the general chaos. Attack every issue with awareness of the whole and how it will be affected.

I've met so many managers, producers, and directors who firmly believe that chaos never takes control, which I have come to see as their coping mechanism for keeping themselves sane (that's straight-up denial, for the uninitiated). Even with their beautiful project plan completely on fire they still think everything's just fine. I believe this is similar to a mother forgetting the pain of childbirth and desiring to go through the process again for child number two. When all is said and done, you really have to go with the flow no matter how many obstacles appear and remember that you need to stay positive, focusing at all times on what can be done instead of what can't. Every day you can only do what you can in the limited time you are given. Just keep a weather eye on the final dates and work toward that destination.

Steps to Success

- Learn to give up your control of the project and know—not think, know—that it will get there in the end. Now recite that like a mantra in the closet with a bottle of booze ... I won't judge.
- The next time your plans are completely ruined, recite this line and smile: "*I never did mind* about the *little* things."
- The better you understand how chaos influences games, the better an employee you will be at any company, because no matter where you go, chaos is always there. The ones who can ride the waves are the ones who succeed.

PRODUCTION: KEEP IT STABLE

The Point

It sounds like common sense, but keeping the build of the game stable should be your guiding star, as well as the teams'.

Further Definition

The goal should always be to keep the version of the game at any point during development as stable as you can. This means checking and rechecking your changes before they are committed to the code to avoid breaking the game. Buddy checks by other designers is also a great way to make sure that you are not interjecting buggy code into the main version of the game. This will start off as something very difficult in the early days of development, but as more stability is added it becomes something everyone comes to expect. If the build is not stable by alpha, you are in real jeopardy of missing your other dates and launch. Therefore, the earlier you can make this a priority, the better you and your team will be able to make your milestones.

If you're wondering why this is so important, well, I'll tell you. Keeping a stable version lets the entire team develop and commit code to it daily, which means that the build of the game is evolving. If the build is broken, it affects not only you but the entire team. Believe me when I say this: a single wasted day across a whole team is disastrous for any project plan. Plus, when the team is down, they will have to develop off of an older, more stable version of the game, which can have its own issues that might trump your work when it's stabilized. Added to this, the work that builds up on these off days can have a greater negative impact when finally checked in—the larger the check-in, the more bugs it will bring with it, bringing the build down again. Small regular check-ins on a stable build allow for a stable main build of the game for everyone to access so the team can use the build as they need to. I can also say from experience that check-ins right before a milestone are very dangerous to the stability of a milestone build. If you need to show off progress or meet a deadline, you should have a responsible freeze window before the milestone if possible to guarantee a solid offering. Missing a milestone because of a broken build can sometimes mean the difference for a company being paid or a project going forward.

I once heard of an artist who used to build a massive textured sphere into every level they were building. In the art program it had no effect, but in the game build it bogged down the level to the point where it wasn't even playable with the frame rate. He would let this haunt everyone for a while, forcing everyone to work harder to try and figure out how to improve the frame rate. Just before the milestone he would remove the sphere, making the level run beautifully, and everyone would celebrate him as their savior. When I asked why he did it, he said it got everyone to work harder without sacrificing the art—normally the first thing cut down—which he couldn't abide.

Steps to Success

- Learn to check and recheck your work before it's complete.
- Learn to ask for help checking your work. Buddy checks help.
- The first time the build is broken, chip in to help fix it.

PRODUCTION: FRIENDS MAKE LIFE BETTER

The Point

Without others around, any designer is prone to fall down the slippery slope of failure with only their own head to deal with.

Further Definition

From what I've found, most video game developers are introverted by nature. They are the people who many wondered what they would do with themselves when they got out of school without the forced sense of community and social norms. I don't mean to say that this is everyone in games—it's just a common archetype. Introverts by nature are very poor at interacting with others, which leads them to having very few friends, if any. I'm here to tell you that having valued others in your life is a special thing.

Now, by no means am I advocating that you become something you are not or the life of the party, as the party is a fleeting event. I am instead trying to get you to understand that having the right friends can mean the difference between a sorrowful life and a grand adventure worthy of song. The right positive people can raise you up from the person you think you are, hold your hand when the world has beaten you down, and are there to make you think about life in a different way. It's important to seek them out, make time for them, and treasure your time with them. Coupled with this, learn to identify key friends who bring you light in the dark places. It's better, I have found, to have a few great best friends instead of a field of acquaintances who only care about you for a short time. A best friend will be there to sort out what happens come what may. When you're developing games where all your attention will be on the game, you need to feel human after a day of designing. I can't stress this enough—friends have saved me time and time again from total depression. Like everything else friendship takes practice. It won't always be perfect and will need to grow over time.

On a side note, learn the delicate art of removing negative people from your life and being okay with that. You need to recognize that these people are closer to vampires than humans, and they are sucking energy from your life. Strive to be a giver and surround yourself with people who do the same. Takers are better left out of your life—never give them another thought, as they do not deserve your attention. It's a hard skill to learn, and I have seen many wonderful people be brought low by takers. I always ask myself one simple question when dealing with people: Are you adding to my light or taking from it? While possibly impolite, it saves me from being taken advantage of here and now as well as in the long run.

Steps to Success

- Go to a social venue and strike up a chat with a stranger.
- Call that friend you haven't seen in a while and spend quality time with them. It will be worth it.
- Ask yourself what makes you of value and use that knowledge to meet people.

CHAPTER 5

Alpha

CONTENTS

Level 5: Alpha 114
Alpha Definition 116
Alpha: Bugs 118
Alpha: 125% 119
Alpha: Importance of 100% Fix Rate 120
Alpha: The Art of Bug Balance 122
Alpha: Test the Game! 123
Alpha: Ask for Help 125
Alpha: Marathoner vs. Sprinter 126
Alpha: Help Others 127
Alpha: Overtime Madness 129
Alpha: The Sacred Art of the Pivot 130
Alpha: Love QA, Don't Hate Them 132
Alpha: Oh, It's New, We Should Do That 133
Alpha: Updating Design Rather than Getting the Game Done 134
Alpha: Build a Following 136
Alpha: Demos, aka Pure Evil 137
Alpha: Get It Out Early 138
Alpha: Remember *You* in All of This 140

LEVEL 5: ALPHA

As you look out across this level, you will be met with a singular sight. A boundless field of bug monsters as far as you can see all look at you in unison like you're the interloper in their world. This view would humble anyone no matter what skill level and can make the best of us all run screaming together. It looks like many of them have even combined to make larger monsters you never thought possible. Worst of all, through the sea of evil you can spot a really small gate in the distance and once again those quality allies are there ready to judge you.

Instead of hanging up your gear and walking away, you have to defeat these little beasties. This means formulating a plan every day to clear out as many sections as you can, remembering that the blighters will crop up again in places you thought were already clean. It's an exhausting journey in this level, but you're not alone—your allies will also stand by your side to vanquish the evil that beset this land. The best you can hope for is to take out as many big ones as you can, for there is never enough time to eradicate them all. You are permitted to curse the mission timer, though, from time to time.

This is the moment they speak about in myths and fables where you have the ultimate showdown against everything you have done. All your sins and virtues are laid bare for everyone to see, and you must face the collective evil, as they must all be dealt with before success can be claimed. This showdown will see its peak, it will reach the sky, and then in the next moment it will start to diminish if you have fought well. Just remember that you're there to kill them, not create more through your actions, which means you must stay ever vigilant. When you finally see the cresting of the waves of monsters, this is not the time to let up. Quite the opposite, it's the time to pour on the steam, powering through the last of them in the knowledge that one day there will be none left.

On the way down to the gate, over a hill of bug monsters, you will have a cathartic moment where you finally see the end of the game in view. It will be a flicker of hope and you will know this game can be finished against all odds. It's a wonderful and horrible moment—you can see success, yet there is an impossible amount of work left to do. There are many more stories to live through and time to tell them when the day is done. Take heart that you have gotten this far.

After you've bled on the battlefield, sacrificed more time than you care to count, and your allies have done the same, you have the chance to reach the great Beta gate. A small door is flanked with those quality judges waiting for the group to arrive where they will again hold your actions in weight against quality. Like your Alpha gate entrance, this too can be a harrowing experience that you face daily. They will send you back to destroy the last of the bugs if they deem you unworthy of making it through. When you finally do make it through, they will give you another part to the robot you have been dragging around, along with entrance into the beta level. You're sure the Robot part will fit at one point, but you just can't see it right now.

ALPHA DEFINITION

The Point

The fifth period of a games cycle is called alpha. This is where everything is implemented into the game and testing is in full swing before beta can be met.

Further Definition

During alpha, designers have anywhere from medium to massive amounts of work to do to make it to beta. By definition, alpha means every feature in the game is present and ready for testing. This doesn't mean they are completed, polished, or refined … just present. It's very good to have that distinction, as something can be there but fail to properly function. There have been times I have been hanging over the shoulders of QA to make sure I hit my alpha date on time, and I did this because even a single day off the dates can cause a final ship date to slip. This could cause my game to miss all of its targeted marketing—without marketing, your game is as good as dead and that can be millions in lost revenue—and be destined for the bargain bin. (If you haven't figured it out yet, everyone should fear the bargain bin.

All in all, though, alpha means bugs and lots of them. QA and the team will fill your issue database full of issues on every part of the game, causing your eyes to do the animated slot machine routine all day every day. As alpha goes on and you're properly fixing your issues, you will begin to notice a significant drop-off of new bugs and workload as you near beta, at which point you basically turn into a glorified, overpaid über-tester. It's not a bad gig and can really be a service to the QA effort, since you know every inch of the product. If you don't know every inch of the product, you have missed reading previous chapters. Go back and learn every inch of your product. Be prepared for many late night shifts, many really poor overtime meals, when the sight of pizza makes you sick and you crave a salad as you cannot remember when you last had one. Coupled with that you will work through more weekends than you thought possible, which takes a real toll on your social life. All of this is for the greater good of the product and meeting the dates on time to hit the proper release window for the market. At least, that's what you should keep saying to yourself when you haven't seen friends, loved ones, or the outside world in months. Alpha is a major achievement and should be treated as such when you make it.

Steps to Success

- Learn to stop making solid plans during this period as they will almost always fall apart. Take the changes in stride. No screaming allowed, and get outside whenever you can.
- Never, ever book a vacation between alpha and final. As I have learned, don't bother until you know you have 100% downtime.
- Realize that home is a state of mind and that work is your home for this duration. As you'll never get to see anyone else, your coworkers are as close as family and should be treated well to survive it.

ALPHA: BUGS

The Point

Bugs will always happen. No matter how great your design is, bugs will arise to haunt you and become a major part of your life as you get further into the production cycle.

Further Definition

By alpha, bugs take up a majority of your day in discussion, evaluation, and fixing them. Learn to love the bug. It will help you refine your product to a state of near perfection and be the greatest tool for your scheduling during the alpha to beta period. Most of the time when you look into your folder in the bug database, you'll see a mound of bugs that have been sent to you from every person you know. It's *Panic, Part V: The Panic Strikes Back*. Again, say this out loud: DON'T PANIC! It's normal. No matter how many bugs there are, you will have to deal with them just like you deal with your design—break them down and systematically conquer them. To do this, you need a method, and after too many years to count dealing with bugs, I have a few secrets to get you through.

First, knock off all of the "need more information" issues, as your answers will help others get to their work faster. Second, sort through all of your issues from ugliest to simplest and group issues that happen in similar areas (such as front-end screen bugs). Third, fit these areas into a quick schedule for what you want to achieve that day, with the judgment that the uglier the bugs are, the more time they will typically take to solve. Fourth, chart your next few days out using the same system. Chaos reigns more than ever during this period, so one to three days is probably the most you can really schedule. Finally, attack each group according to your schedule. This method keeps you on track, lets others know what you're up to when asked, and actually lets you finish each day with success. There will always be more bugs, which forces the unholy feeling that you have never succeeded in a day. It's good to have a mental success point for the end of each day to remind yourself that you're doing great things. Plus, this will keep you sane, which I can tell you is hard when you are constantly trying to chip away at a bug mountain that just keeps getting bigger in the alpha period. Take heart—the mountain can be conquered! And when you're on the other side of it and the bug numbers are decreasing, it will feel that much better.

Steps to Success

- Learn to group like-minded bugs together. There is nothing worse than working through an area only to find you missed a whole bunch of issues, forcing you to go back and thus never feeling like you have finished anything. Bundle and destroy.
- Schedule your time, but always account for a 25% chaos factor that will always happen when you're dealing with people and unforeseen problems.
- If you need to figure out which grouping is more important than another, quickly talk to your lead or production person to find out what they think is more important. If you're still stumped, start at the beginning of the game and work your way to the end, as many players will play your game but not all will finish it.

ALPHA: 125%

The Point

You can always fix more bugs in a day … and when 100% won't do, go to 125%. Yes, I understand that no one can do 125%, but like the old proverb 1 + 1 = 1, you need to open your mind to new possible ways of looking at situations. You may not know it yet, but 125% is doable.

Further Definition

This concept of 125% goes along the lines of you can be better and you can help the game be better every minute of every day. Every time you think you can get your schedule of bugs dealt with, add in a few more on top of that to really show your worth. Some of the best junior designers I've seen who turn into design leads start this from day one and never stop doing it. The funny part is they typically end up in a feast-or-famine situation with bugs. They attack a group of issues with such zeal that they end up finished before everyone else, leaving them primed for more issues. On more than one occasion I have seen designers sitting in the quality assurance department just waiting for bugs to come in to cut down on the lag time to enter them, because they can sometimes deal with them faster than they can be documented.

The 25% guideline is a time-tested technique that not only shows everyone in your group/company that you're a great worker. It also gives that personal added level of satisfaction at the end of the day with a job well done. The real test to this guideline is if you can get it sorted in the time you have without having to stay overtime to accomplish it. No matter what, overtime happens, and you will be in the thick of it by the alpha period. But if you finish your bugs with 25% on top of it that should show you it's time to head for home. This doesn't mean that the 25% has to be all hardcore crash bugs. They can really be a combination of quick-fix issues that you add to the list of your must-fix bugs for the day. Every rule, like guidelines, is made to be broken, and no one rule suits every situation, so learn to know when it applies to you. This means if you have a personal commitment outside of work to get to, then that day you might not need to accomplish 125%.

I realized early on in my career that bugs took on a larger than life role, and if I was going to continue to do well I was going to have to give way more than I ever thought was possible to survive. The real test for me—and for you—is to finish with a super-über feeling of accomplishment and leave the building every day even when you're in bug hell. Easier said than done, I know, but it's something to work toward, which makes it of value.

Steps to Success

- Set yourself a goal of bugs to be fixed. Now add one to three bugs extra to your daily workload to see if it can be done.
- Work your way up to 10% more the following week. See if you can do this in a typical workday, remembering to account for chaos time.
- Work your way up to 15% to 25% and get them all sorted in a regular day.

ALPHA: IMPORTANCE OF 100% FIX RATE

The Point

A 100% fix rate should be your goal every time you submit a bug back to the fix pile. Sounds simple. Sounds like something you can do in your sleep with one arm tied behind your back. Well, I'm here to say, like any art this takes time, focus, and repetition with a strong change log system in place to accomplish.

Further Definition

This is even more important than the amount of bugs fixed, because if you didn't fix the issue properly the first time it's going to come back to you over and over again. That wastes everyone's time and pisses off about every person forced to look at the issue. You have to make your work perfect or as close to that as is humanly possible, knowing that software perfection exists only in coders' dreams at night. No matter how hard you try, there will always be misunderstandings from the bug to the written word to the fix and finally the fix review. Your job is to focus on making the issue flawless, and 100% fix rate is exactly that.

I've known teams where one of the items they were judged on for their bonuses was their individual and group fix rates, and I think that's a very fair assessment of success as it guarantees solid builds of the game throughout development. This proviso in their bonuses actually had a bonding effect on the team and got everyone to help double-check and triple-check their work with others before submitting it to the central game data branch. I've found over the years one of the best ways to guarantee this 100% is to use the buddy check system. As soon as you have your bugs fixed, ask a coworker to check them on your machine and their machine before they are submitted into the mainstream of data. This will give you a double-check most of us really need as well as another fresh pair of eyes that can help you make the fix solid (even if it didn't happen with the first check you did). Plus, sometimes the language of the bug itself can be interpreted differently by another person and can actually help you get to the root cause instead of stumbling around in the dark when you think you have the answer. It's always better to be safe than sorry when interpreting bugs. The buddy system also allows the other designers to know exactly what is going into the game, allowing for another double-check when performing tests of their own. When you get to see all of the fixed bugs going in, you will have a greater understanding of the product as it's being reshaped for final. (Yes, bugs can sometimes reshape design, so the more you know bugs, the more design of your product you know.)

Steps to Success

- Start a buddy system for your design (even hardcopy design applies here) with someone you trust to check over your work.

(Continued)

- When alpha strikes, learn to always ask for a buddy check as you are about to submit your work, and make time to buddy check others.
- The next time you're bounding through your game, look around for the fix you buddy checked for someone else to make sure it got into the main product.

ALPHA: THE ART OF BUG BALANCE

The Point

Fixing all critical bugs doesn't always make a game better. You need to balance the quality of the design against the criticality of the game itself.

Further Definition

Now, most senior designers, managers, and producers will scoff at this idea of balance when they see the massive amount of bugs. They will want you to take care of the most critical bugs first, but that isn't always the best course of action for the game. You must learn to abstract yourself from the language of critical bugs and look at bugs holistically for how they impact players. Many times this nuanced view of bugs gets lost in the paper pushing that is the nature of bugs in software, but it's just as important. Think of it as learning taking off the blinders that the bugs system puts on you. The wider you can expand your view for the entire game's quality, the better you will be at improving the game.

I learned this firsthand on one of my first projects. A senior designer came to me in alpha and asked if the bugs I fixed that day made the game better. Without missing a beat, I answered, "Yes, all of the bugs I fixed had an impact." He chuckled and went through each of my bugs (which were generally high-priority bugs) analyzing each of them with me. In the end he showed me that I had taken care of the worst bugs in my queue but not the ones that had the greatest player impact. They were serious but only in certain specific areas. What he was teaching me was that I needed to look at all my issues holistically instead of knocking out the worst ones first. What fixes had the greatest impact? The next day I started looking at the entire backlog for the bugs that had the greatest impact for the player and not the software itself. This had me fixing issues normally relegated to the low-priority pile and ones that might be shipped by the production team. As most were small, this allowed me to fix many of them fast, and after a week it was remarked that the design had made leaps and bounds as the creature-comfort fixes I made were noticed by many members of the development team. This is how I learned the art of bug balance, and I have never forgotten it. Learn that player impact is an important thing to look at.

Players, I have found, can gloss over areas that have issues but will fixate on something that truly drives them crazy if they see it constantly. This isn't always the case, but ironing out the issues that haunt players on a regular basis in the game—rather than that one specific critical issue in that area of a level that most only visit once for two minutes—is the best course of action. All of this said, sometimes the balance lines up. It's up to you to know when it does and, if the scales are tipped to one side, how to equal them out.

Steps to Success

- Look at the wall and speak out loud what you see. I'll wait.
- Realize that you're seeing with blinders and you don't need too.
- Create balance in your life; equal out your rough spots. If you have traits you know to be detrimental, start making them better.

ALPHA: TEST THE GAME!

The Point

Test the game … test the game … TEST THE GAME! Do it now and don't stop doing it. The tests you create can help find bugs no one ever thought existed. Designers are the most intimate with the product, ergo they are the best at seeing errors.

Further Definition

A friend of mine who was a test manager had a ritual that he would perform on new testers on their first day in the office. He would come into the test area looking as intimidating as possible. Then, as if his physical demeanor didn't scare new people enough, he would scream, "EYES ON SCREEN! TEST THE GAME!" Then he would pick out the most frightened tester and rip into them about how they didn't know anything about testing a game (which was and is very true on your first day). He would wander from scared face to scared face picking up controllers and throwing them around like a madman. Eventually exasperated, he would exit the area in a huff, leaving behind him the indelible memory of fear. He performed this ritual as a joke, and anyone who had been through it tried really hard to keep a straight face. Yet there was method in his madness, as it always had a galvanizing effect on the new testers and made a shared experience to relate to each other about. He told me that as the years went by those in each group carried forward like a military unit that could take on the world together—like basic training with a sergeant who yelled at you for not polishing your boots helped you win a war.

This falls into the category "it's so crazy it just might work." In late production you should be testing the game whenever you are not fixing bugs. I don't care what level of hotshot designer you are or how much you think testing might be beneath you, the game needs to be tested to be finished. If someone on your game team is not testing the game, you can pretty well tell they are there for the paycheck and care very little for the product. By alpha, you really should be the grand master of your game and know every area that currently has issues and what you can chip in to help out the testing effort. I've always heard it said and it's never truer than at this stage of development: designers make the best testers because they know every aspect of the game. If you don't have this knowledge, then you really need to get into testing every area you may have not touched to become a master. If it looks wrong to you, it's a bug. Write it up. The game will be better for it. (Insert very loud screaming voice here: "TEST THE GAME!")

Steps to Success

- Talk to your testing staff about what's wrong in the game when you have the spare time. They will love you for this.
- Get the test plan from QA and go through it when you have the time.
- Write up bugs into a bug database no matter how odd they seem. Everything needs to get into the bug database because it's down to the producer to ship anything, not the designer.

ALPHA: ASK FOR HELP

The Point

When you are faced with an issue you don't know how to fix, take fifteen minutes to try to figure it out. If that hasn't worked, ask for help from someone who might know more. There is no point in wasting your time.

Further Definition

It may sound simple, but you would be amazed how many designers do not ask for help when they are in trouble with work. I think it has to do with the game designer personality type, which is obsessed with figuring out how to make things work. Game designers are puzzle solvers and can on many occasions fall into a puzzle that eats them whole, taking up valuable time. I call this the "architect complex," where the creator of a thing cannot remove their preconceived thought patterns about a subject of their making to look at it from an alternative or outside point of view. This means you have to actually ask another member of the team who might know more than you for help and accept the idea that you are not godlike. Yes, I know your bruised ego doesn't like it, but it's something we all as humans need to learn. You don't need to ask for help right away every time, but it should be done sooner rather than later. The two hours you spent trying to figure out an issue while the guy/gal beside you could have shown you in five minutes equals time *you* wasted for the sake of your ego. Not only that, you also managed to waste time you could have been spending doing more for the game, which sucks.

I used to watch my junior designers closely to see if they were taking too long on an issue. If they were, I would scoot my chair over to offer my help or get them to explain what they were doing in detail, under the guise of just wanting a status update. This approach gave their ego an out, but they really had to learn to ask for help. I typically judged it on a case-by-case and person-to-person basis. Coupled with this, you also need to acknowledge the person for helping you, as they have taken time out of their already busy day to help you solve this problem. That's their chaos time you're creating, so you need to offer them respect for allowing you to be the chaos. Plus, people love helping and a kind word of appreciation goes a long way. I used to actually grade my designers on this and put it into their yearly reviews because it's such an important trait to have. No matter how much you think you know every part of the game, you don't know it all, and the sooner you accept that learning from others is going to make you a better person, the sooner your career will skyrocket.

Steps to Success

- Ask someone on the street for directions even if you live there. This will help teach you how to ask anyone for help in a safe, controlled way.
- Ask a coworker for help in the first thirty minutes of working on an issue.
- Ask a coworker for help on something in the first five to ten minutes. The faster you get to this place, the better employee you will be. Always remember to offer kind words of thanks to the one who helped you.

ALPHA: MARATHONER VS. SPRINTER

The Point

There will always be times in the development cycle when you will be expected to sprint to a milestone—and as milestones get added, you might feel like that's all you do. Yet it's best to learn to be a marathon runner whose steady pace wins the race.

Further Definition

I'm sure you are aware of the classic tale of the tortoise and the hare. The crafty bunny thinks his speed is everything but eventually is outwitted by the slow-moving tortoise. Well, in games it's very similar to this story—the hares tend to die off quickly with the tortoises surviving in the industry for years to come. This doesn't mean to say that there aren't periods when a hare's speed is called for to get a milestone completed. You just need to know when to hit the gas instead of going full throttle the whole time. Don't be the bunny but be of the bunny (you see what I did there?).

I worked with a group of producers who started doing overtime in the development phase of the project, working many hours each evening even when the game was barely functional. They did this for six months straight on the way to the game's release. Most stayed because of social perception—they wanted to be seen as great employees who supported the game. By the time we got into alpha the group was useless and couldn't make a call if their lives depended on it. It was at this point that I started working overtime to support the product and team. The funny part was that I was actually picking up tasks they were supposed to be doing. Their output had decreased so much they could barely handle their day job, let alone overtime.

After about a month of overtime the game was finished, and we worked a few weekends to hit the launch dates. Those producers didn't even show up for the weekend days. After the game launched, the leader of the game gave out reward days to make up for the overtime we had done, and I received the same as all of the producers (the maximum number, I'll have you know), much to their disdain. They spoke up immediately about how much more work they had done than me and how they deserved more time off. I kept uncharacteristically quiet, and the leader explained that I was there when they needed it instead of those who burned themselves out before the finish line. The lesson of the tale: know when to be the hare but live your life like the tortoise. They have a happier existence.

Steps to Success

- Put together a one-page pitch with only one hour for its completion. (Note: This is also fun to do with a group of designers, as the results are often great.) Realize it's more fun to make a pitch without the time limit.
- Turn off distractions around you or limit your exposure to them to focus your day's work on getting a consistent amount of work completed.
- When asked to do overtime, don't let social pressure control you. Judge the need yourself and know that the better person will know when to do overtime.

ALPHA: HELP OTHERS

The Point

When you have a spare moment (and the ability) to help answer a question for someone else, take that time and offer that support. The help you give today could be the life preserver you need tomorrow. As you mature as a designer, you will notice that you spend more of your time—or at least, you should—supporting others rather than actually affecting the game itself. The help you give is for the benefit of the game as a whole.

Further Definition

On the flip side of asking for help, I used to try to instill the trait of offering help into my designers from day one by forcing them to jump through hoops for every other team member before they could work on their own projects. In the end, every one of them had a check system with each other that asked pointed questions about how they were handling their assigned areas. It was great because by alpha everyone on the team knew everyone else's areas, and the minute someone took a sick day any member of the design team could jump in to fix bugs that needed to be done for the next build we sent out. This is especially good because people react differently to overtime and could fall down when you need them the most. Knowing as much as possible about each other's work can be a lifesaver.

Offering your help when you have completed your own work shows everyone around you that you're doing great and is a trait really noticed by managers. Once I was sitting in the design office during alpha and a manager came in to see what was going on that day. I was the only one present, which caused him to fly into a rage over the others not being at work or fixing bugs. After I calmed the poor man down, I explained that all of their bugs had actually been dealt with that day, doubled-checked, and put inside the game for testing. As further explanation, I related that one of the design teams on a sister product was in desperate need of editing feedback and playtest evaluators, and our team had volunteered to help as their plates were clean. The greatest need was not our current game but the sister game, even though our game was in alpha. I'm sure you're saying, "Hey, you just said I should be testing when I have spare time!" Well, it's really a learned skill to gauge which area is most in need of your services, whether it's in quality assurance or design assistance. It takes many project cycles to have this skill become second nature, so don't worry if you haven't gotten it in the first cycle. Personally, I take a huge amount of pride in helping people and feel like it's something that takes a certain level of stress off my team, which I think everyone in this world should be demonstrating both in and out of work. Give selflessly.

Steps to Success

- Offer to help someone crossing the street or aid them in getting their groceries home. Be a Good Samaritan where possible.

- Offer to help someone at work and learn their area.
- Set up a system of checking with every member of your team to help them out. Then add other disciplines if you have that experience.

ALPHA: OVERTIME MADNESS

The Point

Most (if not all) companies and projects require some form of overtime to meet a date or milestone. You need to figure out how best to deal with the dreaded OT madness.

Further Definition

Now, to be frank, overtime is the result of one thing. Some project manager set up a schedule that didn't account for extra work that needed to be completed or the chaos inherent in game development. The result is the dates need to be made and the staff has to suffer to get the job done. I still find it amazing that project managers or whoever sets the schedule never get judged on this. It's a sad state that I can say over the years has improved across the industry (it's not gone by any means, but it is improving). The fact is that eight-hour workdays at an average of forty hours a week has been proven to be the sweet spot for people being able to deliver the most profitable amount of work. Not everyone is the same, but on the whole it works for the masses. Over my many years of watching overtime, I have seen amazing games get saved from not making their release, yet at the same time I have seen stupid bugs get added, poor calls made, and staff lives ruined too. It's a slippery slope that most companies take advantage of, which means you need to decide what is best for you.

If you are going to start to do any overtime, I suggest the following ideas to keep you sane during it. First off take a five to ten minute break every two hours and get away from your work desk to relax your mind and recharge. During feeding times, eat away from your desk and if possible get outside for some exercise. Healthy body, healthy mind. If your work is done for the day, leave even if others are doing OT, no matter what guilt you get handed about it. It's pointless to sacrifice yourself for another person's perception of you being at your desk. If possible, try to have weekends off—they are the best traditional way to recharge your mind as well as motivate yourself to attack the next week's work with fervor. These helpful hints have helped me, but there are dozens more to help make the madness bearable.

Overtime is madness, but if you learn to treat whatever comes at you properly on your terms rather than the ones set up for you, it will serve you better in the long run. A clear, rested mind solves problems faster for the benefit of everyone involved. Don't sacrifice yourself for one game when your mission should be to survive for a career of games. When you start to look at it that way, it makes going home at the right time that much easier and guilt free.

Steps to Success

- Come up with three to five ways to improve your workday when doing overtime.
- Figure out what the optimum work week looks like for you where you are producing positive work. Then use that to base your work/life balance on. Surprisingly, it might not be forty hours a week.
- Stand up for yourself and say, "I will not do overtime" if you do not think it is needed. Learn to not let others guilt-trip you.

ALPHA: THE SACRED ART OF THE PIVOT

The Point

It's not enough to be focused. You also have to learn to pivot at a moment's notice to focus on another area, feature, and even game. Think of it not like running a race but gearing up for a game of tag.

Further Definition

The ability to attack situations, problems, and goals independent of each other is a feat that many designers fail to ever learn, yet it's something that would do everyone in the profession a great service. I call it the sacred art of the pivot, where one can simply pivot on one heel, swing around, and carry on running in another direction. An oversimplified view I grant you.

On many occasions throughout a project a designer will be asked to change focus to evaluate another part of the design. This requires the designer to drop their current priorities, headspace, and thought patterns to support another area for the company and the game. I myself have succeeded and failed at this. It's not enough to change your actions. You must also change your headspace to help the greater design effort, which is very difficult. If you have been focused on a specific feature for months and are one day asked to put together a new pitch for another game, it can be hard to shake off the remnants of the former task to support the next one. Plus, you also have to emotionally accept this chaos in your routine, which many people do not do well.

Over the years I have heard many fine designers say that they can change tack at a moment's notice but when put to the test many fail to even pull themselves out of the headspace they are in with their current priorities. That's not to say that they can't do this, it's just a skill like any other and requires practice. Many think that flexibility is just part of their personality and a natural skill—you either have it or you don't—but that's a load of misinformation. Skills take practice, practice is hard, and hardship breeds success later down the line.

That said, the best piece of advice I can offer is that you have to be ready every hour to do something different. You are not someone on an assembly line who performs the same actions endlessly every day until they hear the whistle blow. The more you can compartmentalize yourself on short notice, the more valuable you will be as a designer. If you cannot figure out how to switch your headspace, I suggest getting away from your desk for five minutes. Go outside, sit, sketch, listen to music with your eyes closed, or anything else that in a small way breaks up your current focus to allow you to accept new stimulus in to get the job done.

Steps to Success

- Select four separate actions, two physical, two mental. Set yourself two minutes for each and jump back and forth between them.
- Now select two hobbies that involve logic and two that involve the arts. Set yourself one hour for each and jump back and forth between them for an evening.
- Spend an hour creating something. Then destroy it and be okay doing it.

ALPHA: LOVE QA, DON'T HATE THEM

The Point

From alpha to final, quality assurance are quite possibly the most valuable members of a game team—and historically the least respected. It should be your job as a designer to help push them to greater heights and not knock them down because they dream of being you.

Further Definition

It's a sad state of affairs, but QA is still largely seen as just a bunch of kids who play games without having a clue how to develop them. They are the traditional unskilled workforce in the eyes of many. That is a load of crap and should be scrubbed from your head—these people are going to help you guarantee a great product. Now, I know that QA is the group that brings up all of the flaws about your game, detailing every separate occurrence, and that this causes you to work ungodly hours to make sure the issues are sorted out. On paper, all of this would make anyone start planning their deaths—hopefully metaphorically, not literally. Yet this isn't the whole truth. These wonderful people are the gatekeepers to a successful product, as you've seen for any AAA game. A few horrible bugs can destroy the sales of a whole game even though thousands of bugs were fixed to ship the game.

First off, you need to listen to these people, as they see with eyes unclouded by development concerns. Second, they are there to make sure the game is at its highest quality level. That's their job. Third, they are the last line of defense that will need to sign off on the game before it goes to manufacturing for consumers. This means it's a really good idea to make friends with them, visit them, and discuss things with them on a constant basis. A little friendly communication could help you later on when you get hundreds of bugs that could have been avoided with a quick conversation.

One company I worked at used to have Friday beers bought by the company for the development staff, which was everyone in the company except QA. As these people worked just as hard as anyone else in development, I used to walk into the party and sneak a six-pack to bring to QA. And I will tell you, nothing is worth more than the look on their faces when they see you showing them respect (especially breaking the rules for them beer respect). Understand that most of them would love to have your job, which means they look up to you. You can be the person worth looking up to, and that means you need to love them.

Steps to Success

- Visit QA and chat about any old thing a few times a week.
- Offer the QA team an open-door policy to ask you questions. (If the team is too large, offer this to a few you think are top notch.) You will be a star in their eyes.
- Bring them presents (food, candy, beer) when overtime hits. They are typically underpaid compared to you, and it shows you care about them doing a great job. Beer on an OT Friday or weekend means more than you will ever know.

ALPHA: OH, IT'S NEW, WE SHOULD DO THAT

The Point

The games industry is fickle and switches direction on a dime. What's in fashion can change with one game, so you must be prepared for your design to change with that fashion trend.

Further Definition

All games take time to create, during which time things can change, and I can assure you they will. Your design that you created with the blessing of everyone involved is now outdated by a newer piece of software on the market. This is an age-old problem that every designer has had to face. Do you jump to the latest new thing even though it has consequences? Or should you stick to your original guns for the design?

To answer the question truly, you need to do the following and stick to it. First, if something new has changed the gaming landscape, review it like any other feature, objectively. Next, you need to figure out if your team can even make the changes in the time they have to ship the game. Not all teams have this luxury, and if the numbers don't pan out it's an easy decision. If there is space/time to do the new feature, then I suggest bringing in everyone involved to take a vote. This is the only way to get everyone on board and a dictatorial edict will just piss people off. If all of the stars align and the design needs to change to mimic the new shiny, accept it with pleasant humility. There are other battles to fight, but if the call is to stick with it, be confident that everyone helped make that call. Game creation is a team sport and the call doesn't just need to be on one person.

I can still remember the first time a producer walked into a morning meeting on a project exclaiming they had seen the future of games in the title they had played that weekend and we were going to have to rework everything to try to capture some of that magic. That producer forced the call, had everyone play the title, forced a massive rework of the game, which in turn forced overtime, our dates were missed, we missed our ship window for marketing, it was reviewed as a cheap copy of another game, and it only got mediocre sales. The worst part was that all the features in the background from the original design were lauded as spectacular by gamers who questioned openly why they were not the focus. The producer lost his job for that.

On the other hand, I know of teams that refused to change design and they suffered a similar fate of mediocre sales as they were not what the player populace was looking for. It's a difficult call to make. All I can say is treat it as a group call, live with the decision, and keep making games.

Steps to Success

- Look up games that came out after a great original one and tried to mimic its success. How did those copies of the original do fiscally?
- Research the last few years of game trends. Learn that everything changes.
- The next time you have a big call to make, involve others in the decision-making process. Group source your choice.

ALPHA: UPDATING DESIGN RATHER THAN GETTING THE GAME DONE

The Point

Even if it seems like the biggest waste of time and the most ridiculous practice you can think of, spend some quality time to update the design to match the game … yes, even if it's changed drastically.

Further Definition

This is one of the hardest things to do near the end of the project cycle, and I will admit, it's something I loathe doing, as the game will have changed a lot during its development cycle. (Remember that Porsche we designed? Well, now it's a Beetle.) The key thing to remember is that keeping up with the paperwork is going to help QA test your game accurately and give you fewer bugs in the long run. QA uses your design to create its test strategies, which can be ever changing. The real problem is that at this point in the project you really want this game to get done to the best possible standard, and updating documents is pretty much last on your list of things to get done. Seriously, I had cleaning my desk (a warzone of epic disaster that is something akin to a post–World War III trash city) higher on my priority list than updating my design—that is, until the fateful day I got handed a host of bugs that were not bugs. The design had changed, but QA didn't know about it. Suddenly my desk stayed messy and I cared about updating documentation.

I have been beating into you that the game is your true priority, and that means documentation has its place. This is a reminder for you that it's very important and should be something you make sure happens. The best way to keep updates in order is whenever you make a change you know will augment the core of your design documents, write it down in point form in an email, leaving it in your drafts folder to add to later. (Whatever you do, never ever go into my drafts folder. It looks like a six-year-old's room without parental supervision.) When you have the time, take the points and update the design documentation, adding in an editing change log beside the line you have changed along with an email to everyone you believe it will matter to when completed. This double communication—in your design and to the team—will help everyone know what is going on with the product. Plus, it's always important to explain the "WHY" of a change, as most people will undoubtedly disagree with the choice but will be compliant if they know the reasoning behind it. As an added bonus, you will get props from staff and managers for keeping them in the loop. Clean documentation equals a cleaner game.

Steps to Success

- Create an email with the subject line "Design Changes" and leave it in your drafts folder to update with any changes to the design documentation.
- Update this email constantly, crossing off points you have completed. Update your design documentation and remember to update what you have changed.
- Send a daily email with your changes to everyone you think will benefit from it in a quick point-form format, always remembering to add in the "why."

ALPHA: BUILD A FOLLOWING

The Point

The cult of personality is alive and well in our modern culture, which means it's on you to build a group of followers to see your work.

Further Definition

In the days of video game infancy, companies would hide designers away and leave their credits off their work. This was done for many reasons, but in the end, it was about keeping the designers in their place as well as in their jobs making games for that company. This has changed over time, and now designers are followed like directors are for movies for their skill in crafting amazing experiences. While this has unlocked many opportunities, it also comes at a cost, which is now designers have to be their own evangelists. They need to contribute to the masses' preferred consumption of media to get the message out about the game they are creating. This can be insurmountable by many, as they are not accustomed to it, but like many other facets of life, if you break it down you can take control of it more easily.

There are a few base methods (or hooks) to draw people to your shining light. I suggest you focus on the ones where you know you can shine the most, as trying to do them all will undoubtedly kill you. The first hook is the written method, which ranges from short textualized anecdotes all the way up to full-blown stories for websites to host. Second is visual hooks in the form of art and photography, which when done properly with certain programs can stretch your influence out to countless people who follow what you're up to. The last hook is video, which can be anything from a posted video online to being a guest on a television show. These hooks all create conversation with others and spark allegiance if you're selling what the masses want to buy. All of these take advantage of available media routes to expand your name, your brand, yourself. Just remember that working these hooks can take up a lot of time, so it's good to set boundaries to keep it in check. Many a fine designer I've known has fallen into the media trap of focusing just on their media presence. Just remember that and you'll be okay.

Now, why should you spend your hard-won extra time cultivating followers? Well, it's important when you want to get the message out about your game. It doesn't take a mega-marketing campaign anymore to get players hooked on learning more, it just takes you (and your time). Just remember to be honest as people are very savvy to frauds. Be the designer you want to project in your social media. With all of this said, also be very careful with what you put out into the world. The Internet doesn't forget, and people rarely forgive. It's important to stay away from acidic people online, rant to your friends rather than a post, and keep your cool when the village idiots come knocking on your metaphorical door. Now, go get those followers.

Steps to Success

- Start a written social media account and post every few days.
- Start a visual media account and let your art speak for itself.
- Record yourself on video and post it. Start conversations.

ALPHA: DEMOS, AKA PURE EVIL

The Point

Everyone who plays games loves demos. No matter how evil they are to develop, you need to give them your focus for the betterment of the product as a whole. In many instances, they are the largest sell of the game you are working on.

Further Definition

Demos are always planned at the wrong time in the development cycle and always end up putting the team into a tight spin on a crash course trajectory to the soft bosom of mother earth. Why then would anyone do this to a team that is already in a crunch period? Well, the answer is simple: PROFIT. Demos are really the best chance the market has to see your product, make their judgments on its viability for purchase, and preorder it.

As an added bonus, the demo can also help a designer refocus on what is and isn't working with the game through online comments, which is extraordinarily helpful in avoiding disaster. Be forewarned, there will be haters, trolls, and Internet goblins who will want to dump on your little piece of glory. You have to learn to sift through for the kernels of wisdom that will appear when you extrapolate the right lessons from it all. Comments from the press and forums can help you refine mechanics to make them sing for the end product. At the same point, though, comments from the players and press can literally force you to rethink areas that you may have thought were in a great place. Use the comments to learn more, and keep your ego out of it no matter the feedback. The worst case is if you have to remake the entire product because a demo has failed, forcing your whole team back into the development phase again, but that will be decided above your pay grade if it happens. The best you can do is take the comments from the demo and act on them accordingly.

I personally think of the little demos as a smaller project cycle on fast forward. They need just as much of your love to get to final. The only real issue is that the demo typically shows up during the development cycle when the code is not final, the art is virtually placeholder, and it's riddled with crippling bugs forcing a massive amount of hacked band-aids to be applied to get it out the door rather than focusing on the game itself getting to final. The demo, like you, will never be perfect, so don't expect brilliance. Just work as hard as you can, remember it's a work in progress, and get it done as fast as possible so you can get back to the main product's needs.

Steps to Success

- Download a boatload of demos and try them out, grading each.
- Take this list and add the best and worst about each of the demos.
- Realize that most demos are not complete and are riddled with issues. Keep this in mind as you try to build one. It's a slice of pie, not the whole pie.

ALPHA: GET IT OUT EARLY

The Point

Most developers and companies are petrified at the thought of putting out a game early, but if done right, early release can make a game amazing.

Further Definition

As technology has advanced, so has the opportunity for games to come out early. Now, why would you send out a game offering at alpha or beta when it has not been completed? Well, it allows you something that most games don't get until launch day: real-world player data. This is a priceless commodity that will allow you and your team to perfect the game before launch.

If the team decides this is a good idea, it's wise to look at exactly what you want to offer for the early-access game, as it will be obtainable at a reduced cost to the players who want to participate. Now the decision is whether to have part or all of the game in the offering (part is normally safer so you don't give up all the cookies in the cookie jar). Once you have the base offering, you can figure out how you are going to track the player in the game and what data they will be able to give you on what they do and any bugs they find. You would be amazed how a player population that demonizes a launch title for minor errors will totally be fine with an early-access title riddled with bugs, because they know they are getting an insider's pass to the show. As a designer, this can be hard because you know the offering is not at its best.

Once you have a plan for what you're going to offer and how it will be tracked it, now comes a quest to put together what is required, like it would be for a demo. A small project plan is organized, and the best rule of thumb for an early-access product is to get the optimum route through the game working. If the player chooses to move away from that desired route, they get what's coming to them (bugs, lots of bugs). Once this basic setup is clear of issues, it's a good idea to set up the launch like it's a real launch day. Once it's live, you will start collecting data and can start listening to players' feedback online, which can greatly help you improve the design before full launch. Do your best to collect all of this data and look at it dispassionately (always easier said than done). Work out with the team any changes that are needed and work tirelessly to get the fixes into the product before it's launched. As an added bonus, you can make updates to the early-access game through patches. These allow the team to communicate online all of the fixes being made for the game. I have learned that players love to be heard. They like being told their feedback is valid, changes are being made in their favor, and it will all be in the final game. If you're lucky the lessons learned from the players in an early-access release will guarantee a higher reviewer rating, a fervent fan base, and increased unit sales.

Steps to Success

- Research games that have done early-access offerings. Learn from them as much as you can as they have been there first.
- Look at games that failed on release that fixed it after.
- Play an early-access title and learn from it. It's not perfect.

ALPHA: REMEMBER *YOU* IN ALL OF THIS

The Point

You are the most important part of your game design. You need to remember to make sure that you stay present instead of becoming a recessive hermit.

Further Definition

It might be surprising to you, but the loss of self in the pursuit of completing a game happens to designers more than you would think. It happens gradually at first, yet as the pressure and the hours start to mount the tendency is to focus on the game instead of on the *you*. If this is kept up, by the end of the project you're a husk of the former you and can barely deal with regular life as it doesn't conform to the game's design. The *you* can be rationalized to wait until later and forced down to make sure that your pursuit comes to fruition. Well, I'm here to say it's time to take a step back and focus on the *you* for fear of losing yourself completely.

This means you need to take positive steps every day to celebrate and honor yourself. These can be the simplest of actions from morning exercise (psst, your health is important to maintaining a well-balanced mind) to dessert after dinner (remember, a sinful dalliance makes life worth living). Over time, my *you* moments per day have changed greatly, and I find that each year I have different desires to support me staying grounded in being me. What I can say from experience is that it's smart to think up a few things each day that best support your *you* needs. If you're having trouble coming up with some, start at the beginning of an average day for you and break out what actions you do to support you staying sane. Once you have a list, make those actions a priority. It takes focus and thought to really come to grips with this, yet when it's in place you will find yourself throughout the day saying internally, "YES! It's me time!" These little celebrations of the *you* will become something that you enjoy daily no matter what is going on. Just a reminder: *you* time doesn't need to be alone. It can be as simple as a conversation with coworkers or friends over a coffee at 3 p.m. when your attention begins to wane.

Now, on the reverse side of this coin, if you don't focus on the *you* there is a great possibility of losing yourself completing a project. This course of action burns you out, leaving you drained and rudderless upon the sea of life. I can remember a designer who burned himself out on the project. He went home one night and tried to use his electronic work pass to get into his house instead of his keys. After repeatedly swiping the card and nothing happening, he started banging on the door demanding to be let in by security. After a moment, he snapped back to reality, realizing that he was at home. He told me he just collapsed crying at the door, knowing he had lost himself. After that, he made a purposeful time every day to get back his sense of self instead of being a mindless automaton that was only wanted for work.

Steps to Success

- Write down ten things you do just for you on a regular basis.
- Figure out what stretch goals can be added to each day and do them.
- Give your attention to you-related activities and moments to reward yourself.

CHAPTER 6

Beta

CONTENTS

Level 6: Beta 144
Beta Definition 146
Beta: Johnny or Janie on the Spot 148
Beta: Check Every Bug Yourself 149
Beta: Know Your Game 150
Beta: Monotony 152
Beta: Play Your Game 153
Beta: Play Where the Player Plays 154
Beta: Herding Cats 156
Beta: Relax—It's in Everyone's Best Interest 157
Beta: Prepare Yourself for Interviews 159
Beta: Love QA Even More 160

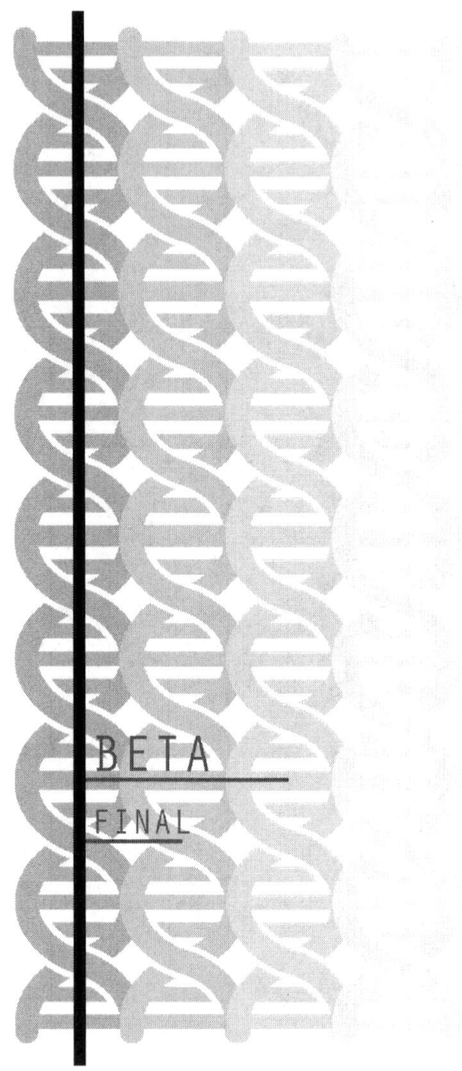

LEVEL 6: BETA

This level is presented to you as the fields you saw in the last level but without the horde of bug monsters inhabiting it. It's a stark world you're not used to, but that will not last for long as bugs will crawl their way up to meet you. You'll have to rush off to meet each one, working in combination with your allies to thwart them. Then you wait until the next call to arms. It's not as exhausting as the last level, but it will test your mettle to stay consistent and finish your mission.

This level will put all you have learned about the game to the test, as the job's not done yet. Even though you will be drained emotionally and physically, you will need to maintain a cool demeanor when fighting the worst issues. With the end in sight, all you want to do is fall over. The best way of dealing with this is to grab rest where you can to refill your health meter and do your best to support your allies. Some of the monsters will conquer themselves without any assistance from you. Bring your allies what they need and when asked to go on a bug hunt be positive, even if it's just canned animation with you giving everyone a thumbs-up with a smile on your face. It helps even if you don't feel it.

The day you awake, pick up your gear ready for the fight, and there is nothing left to do can feel like a resurrection. You have fallen so low with all of this battling. You have lost yourself and who you wanted to be in this game. When there is nothing left to fight, you're left there without armor, shield, or sword, naked for the world to see. You only know how to forge forward to fight, and now you're forced to wait. The waiting can be its own form of torture—you're so used to running on all cylinders that its absence can feel like you're missing a part of yourself. That said, the creatures *will* reappear and you'll need to jump back to action with a level head. It's a feast or famine situation, which is just another puzzle for you to learn to conquer.

Your allies look about as haggard as you feel, with their scars showing and half their armor missing. It's a sad sight compared to the group you started this game with and a clear reminder of how much it takes to get through this. It takes a strong person to handle this work, which no one told you when you started. Respect them for their scars and when possible raise a glass to celebrate each other.

When you have had enough days of no monsters in the level and you have gotten used to the idea that they will never return, you will be met with the gate that appears out of nowhere in the middle of the level. As soon as it appears, so do your quality ally judges to make sure the bar is met. As much as you would like to curse them for being here yet again, you know they want to see the game done as much as you do. At this point, they are there as functionaries to uphold the rules for all those who will enjoy the title. They are the last line of defense and deserving of your respect. When they are satisfied they will bestow upon you the key to travel to the level of final—and a little piece you didn't realize your robot needed. Be gracious and thank them as you pass through this threshold.

BETA DEFINITION

The Point

This sixth period of a games cycle is called beta. This is where everything is pretty much completed in the game, you're fighting the daily zero bug count, and testing is hunting down the last few bugs before final is met.

Further Definition

During beta, designers are pretty much reduced to being those glorified overpaid testers I mentioned before, with workloads that are more on the manageable side. No less stress—just not constant unrelenting stress. By definition, beta is zero major bugs left in the product to be dealt with, and the period averages about two to four weeks. Zero never lasts for long and throughout beta more bugs are found every day, decisions are made about what to do with them and if they are to be fixed or shipped. The goal every day in beta is to leave when there are zero bugs. If that zero sticks for a certain amount of time, you have gotten to final. Now, that is a goal that doesn't always get achieved, but it's at least the focus for everyone to follow. Think of it like a plane trying to make a landing on a windy runway. It touches down on the tarmac a few times before getting everyone safely on the ground. (Hopefully. I have seen some projects' beta look like a crash landing where everyone walked away scarred.)

The last few issues are the real doozies and cause many fine developers to collect around meeting tables discussing how to attack them without causing even more issues. You have to understand that every code change could initiate many more bugs for the one that is going to be fixed. Along with that, it's time for everyone to be testing the game. It feels more like everyone has been drummed into service, press-gang style, to find any bug they can and I do mean EVERYONE.

The best thing to do during this time is stay focused on the game (believe me, you won't want to look at it by this point as you routinely see it in your sleep), test every conceivable way you can think of in the game, and help out wherever you can whenever you can. People who survive this period with a solid head on their shoulders really prove how great a developer they are. I've seen great people crack during this period as they stop seeing the end in sight and instead feel the pressure of every day never staying at zero. You're tired, you're spent, and you're so close to the end. It's time to be extra nice to everyone around you even if you want to eat them alive. A truly great designer lets himself or herself be the solution no matter what happens, and in beta it's doubly important.

Steps to Success

- TEST THE GAME! EYES ON SCREEN! TEST THE GAME!
- Talk to everyone who still has a bug and offer any assistance if they need it, even if that means testing it on the spot.
- Do not snap. Sounds easy, but when you have no brain from sleep deprivation and you haven't seen your loved ones in ages, your fuse is measured in nano-units.

BETA: JOHNNY OR JANIE ON THE SPOT

The Point

You need to be—not learn to be, but *be*—the human on the spot when it's needed. How do you do that? Well, it's simple. Know the product so intimately your lover feels left out, which is easier said than done.

Further Definition

Near the end of the project, your knowledge is one of your most valuable assets. You have been, seen, and done everything around the game. You are a member of the one group that will have touched the most parts of the game. It has turned you into a master whether you know it or not. It's a very true statement that anything a human does for a thousand hours turns them into a master of it.

You will be consulted on many issues and the best way to fix them without causing more knock-on bugs. You have to be ready to share your wealth of experience with anyone who asks and then stand by your decision come what may. Hold on tightly, and let go lightly. Say that last sentence again out loud, it's important. You should take a lot of personal pleasure being the central linchpin and offering your two cents about any issue you're asked about, even if you're not directly going to be fixing it. That's where the "lightly" comes into play—you are not always the decision maker, and you need to be okay if the fix goes against your call. As you approach the end, everyone will want to gather your expertise before making an educated decision on how to go forward. Remember to offer it up freely and without sounding like a know-it-all. The people coming to you are seeking aid, not a judgmental bastard. It's the difference between acting like an encyclopedia and acting like a fanatic with religious doctrine.

I once had an entire team spend four hours arguing over a bug without a clue what to do in the end. I got sick of listening to it and walked over to offer a fresh pair of eyes. After they explained the issue and each of their points, I came up with the answer: simply cut the small area of issue out of the level—it really had no gameplay value anyway—which everyone rejoiced to hear. They were trying hard to shoehorn in a bad situation instead of eliminating it altogether. All of them had forgotten to look outside of the box for an answer. There are times from beta to final when a single word from you can mean the difference between hours of work by multiple staff members and not needing to implement a fix in an area no one will notice. Weigh your choices carefully.

Steps to Success

- Stop in to the production areas to offer your assistance with any bugs.
- Learn to weigh the good of the product against the possible issues that arise because of a fix. This comes with experience, but you should try.
- Learn to offer your advice and then allow the person asking to come to the best conclusion themselves if possible.

BETA: CHECK EVERY BUG YOURSELF

The Point

When time allows, you should be double-checking every fix that goes into the game to make sure for yourself that the fix is solid. This is QA's job, but in beta you will be able to see all the angles with minimal fixes going into the game.

Further Definition

By the time beta has hit, there are precious few bugs left in the game that need to be dealt with daily. Almost all of your time should be spent testing the product (I will hammer this into you until you get it). It's at this point that you really need to review every bug that has a fix submitted for it, and I'm not just talking design-related issues, I mean ALL issues. This handy-dandy routine will give you a greater understanding of what's left to be done in the game before it can be shipped to the consumer. Yes, every game ships with bugs no matter what. This is due to time constraint, but it's still good to know what's being handled now. A thorough issue review will prepare you to give everyone your valuable insight when it matters—when you need to be Johnny or Janie on the spot.

I've had producers call me up in the dead of night to talk about issues because I was the one person who had been through all of them in the game, while other groups just made sure their own issues were covered. They had stopped working after they got their piece of the pie done, not realizing how it affected the entire pie. Because I was the one communicating with them directly about it, I become an unofficial second-in-command to help the producer make decisions on how the issues could be sorted out. This action alone gave me a better understanding of the entire product and how issues might cause other ones to crop up if fixed improperly. The knock-on issue can be a developer's worst nightmare at this point. Understanding how all parts of the game are interconnected is the best way to get it out the door. In the end you should want to be that person who gets that late night call, and like I've mentioned, before your knowledge is priceless. A little extra effort can make all the difference in the long run of a successful game. I understand that at this point checking every bug might be the last thing you want to do—you have been looking at the same game for longer than you care to remember—but it's an important routine that will help your entire team make it to final.

Steps to Success

- Whenever a fix list is submitted into the game in the beta period, check it yourself no matter what department it came from.
- Become intimate with the bugs that are left in the database—know who is fixing them, when they are expected to be fixed, and which ones have been shipped.
- Convince every other designer around you to do the same and spread the work out so that everyone sees what's going on. You never know if you'll be sick and not there to give the helpful answers. The team matters more than your ego's desire to be the savior of the game.

BETA: KNOW YOUR GAME

The Point

Know your game sounds simple enough, but it's actually becoming more difficult as games get larger and open worlds become the norm. If you haven't finished the game more ways than you ever imagined, go back and do it again.

Further Definition

I'm sure you're saying to yourself, "Well, by this point I damn well *should* know my game better than everyone else," but that's not always the case. Many times if you are a junior designer you have been working on a specific area and haven't gotten the chance to really become intimate with all facets of the game. Now is the time to remedy this by diving head first into every area, making 100% completion a mantra.

Going through the game with fresh eyes ("fresh eyes" is a term for looking at a game like it's the first time) is a great way to find convoluted issues you might not have otherwise found. Fresh eyes at this point are a very difficult thing to attain, as you have been over the product (and over it, and over it) and have well-crafted blinders obscuring your view of the game. I have found that imagining what a new user from a different walk of life would do is the best way of gaining fresh eyes. Playing the game just like that is the best way to simulate this fresh perspective without dragging in some hapless victim from the outside world.

You would be amazed what can be found at this point of the production cycle, and on many occasions this has literally saved a product from drastic failure on the market—and I speak from experience on this one. More than once I have found a complex crash bug that my entire team and test team had missed. They were too tied up in verification to get to some truly nasty, deep crash issues. One time when testing a sports product they had a crash in season mode after 117 seasons. As it was almost impossible to fix, they simply capped the seasons at 110 to solve the issue. The simple fact that I had even gone into the product again to try and find anything that deep was massively rewarded by everyone when the game shipped. Treat each run-through like it's a pleasure and something to be relished with as much hooting and hollering as you can muster. Remember, games are supposed to be fun … even at this point.

Steps to Success

- To keep your focus on the product, create a game within the game during a play-through, seeing how many times you can do something no one would ever expect.
- Play the game like it's the first time you have ever seen it (hard, I know). Approach it with fresh eyes like you're someone else with a different agenda for success.
- Try to do things that no one has ever dreamed of doing. Push that philosophy to the extreme wherever you can. Players will, which means you need to.

BETA: MONOTONY

The Point

Sometimes you just have to show up, do the work, survive the day, and return to do it all again tomorrow. It's monotonous, but it's the job.

Further Definition

I can teach you how to see the world from different angles, to think with different thoughts and attack any problem that comes into view. But I cannot teach you how to deal with surviving every day doing virtually the same thing. That is something that everyone must learn to handle for themselves. Whether it's too much work, work without soul, or too little enjoyment, it always leads to the same problem: monotony. There are designers who tackle new and interesting problems every day, yet there is also the designer who spends six months straight on tuning a single weapon. It takes a certain amount of personal gumption to come in every day to do the same general thing without going mad. Heroes aren't always the ones who show up when needed, they are also the ones that are there every day when everything is hard.

From my own experience I have felt like a record on repeat, day in and day out, while developing a game. It's been enough to stop me getting out of bed even though I'm fulfilling my passion by doing design. Over time I learned to recognize the periods of monotony and do something proactive to make sure it doesn't drive me bananas.

First off, I would work to change up my routines. I would walk a different way to work, eat different foods, watch different media, and break habits that seemed to hold me to being powerless by always being the same. If you want to see your world in a new light, all you have to do is take one step off your normal daily path to experience it. Next, I would rather selfishly reward myself with small treats that I didn't need. Anything from sweet treats for the taste buds to items ordered over the Internet. These little items were used as rewards to keep me on track. Finally, I found future goals to keep me motivated and moving forward—something as simple as a movie coming out in six months that I was looking forward to or planning a holiday for after the project was done. These are what I do, but everyone is different. Come up with what you need to do to stay sane.

I included this section as I have seen too many designers go mad in the monotony that no one can train you for. No one teaches you that having this job can sometimes be about just being there every day no matter how repetitive it is. Just keep an even keel on your emotions and come in to work bringing as much light with you as you can. The best we can do is set up ways to survive monotony and come out at the end of it into a positive place.

Steps to Success

- Seriously think about what you will do when monotony strikes.
- Come up with three inventive ways to stave off monotony that work for you.
- Ask others what they do to deal with work when it becomes monotonous.

BETA: PLAY YOUR GAME

The Point

Don't just complete your game, learn to play it just like the new user unwrapping it for the very first time. You are a maker of dreams and entertainment that brings joy to countless people around the world, which means *you* need to see the joy of it.

Further Definition

By this point in the product schedule, you are not the end user who will be playing this game, and as a matter of fact you are probably the furthest removed from that person you will ever be. It's at this time you have to drop everything you thought you knew about the product and start it up like you're a newbie … for fun. I've always found fun a difficult trait to possess by the end of the game. My eyes are so shrouded by complexity I can't see the forest for the trees. The best way I have found to break through this is to watch someone else play the game without any input from me. They will attack the product from a totally different point of view and with different success criteria. After reviewing this play-through I take what I have learned and try the game myself as that person played it. After I'm done, I do it with another person and then another until I'm so used to playing it as different people I've almost lost all of my original style for playing the game.

Another fine method is playing your game from the point of view of different types of players: the hardcore (five to ten hour play-through, trying to do 80% of everything), completionist (don't leave until you have gotten 100%), and casual (bare-bones play style to get through the game in easy two-hour sessions). Different gamer perspectives will open up a host of issues you never expected to find. One time I asked a designer to play the game like a casual user. He played silly for three hours and then left the game running to disappear for lunch. When he returned, he had crashed the product. The crash was caused by leaving the main character in a level that took too much memory to run over time, a level that everyone else had previously just been trying to get through fast. Without trying that player perspective, that issue might never have been found and would end up in the final product. If you don't have access to people inside your company or school, bring in someone from the outside world (nondisclosure agreements signed, of course, or pinky-swears not to release anything) and get them into the product. You will find how many preconceived ideas you have about your game and how it's played will go right out the window.

Steps to Success

- Have someone play the game in front of you and emulate their playing style the next time you play, incorporating what they see as success.
- Bring in someone from outside your group to play the game. Have them give it a whirl so you can see how they attack the game.
- Play the game as a hardcore, a completionist, and a casual gamer. Then come up with three different ways to play it using any archetype you like. Remember, this is fun.

BETA: PLAY WHERE THE PLAYER PLAYS

The Point

People play games these days from the luxury of their homes. If you want to truly get the experience of gameplay with your title, you need to play it at home.

Further Definition

To many this might sound silly or like something that can be overlooked, but if you want to understand the end-user experience, you need to do it in a typical player setting. Living rooms, basements, and home offices are all places where games are routinely played, and learning how the experience will be from that vantage point will help improve your design of the game. You must think about screen sizes, controllers, audio setup, and seating. All of these, while normally not things you can control, can help craft an experience that adds to the player's enjoyment, and you always want to avoid detracting from it.

As an example, I once worked on a four-player multiplayer game. It wasn't until the end of the development cycle that we actually put four players on a couch together to see what would happen when they played in one space, as we had normally run playtests at our desks. The players started messing with controls and buttoning in and out of menus, making it almost impossible to get to gameplay until one player snatched the controllers away from the others. This valuable lesson taught us that to set up gameplay you only needed one player to set up the variables. The extra players only needed to interact with menus to choose what character they wanted to be, which we could unlock when the players got to that screen. This design change made it very easy to control and allowed players to easily get into gameplay in a group setting. We would never have thought of this unless we put everyone in one place together and watched what happened to them.

On another occasion I knew of a sound designer who had worked tirelessly on the audio for the game but had always done it from her desk with headphones on. The moment we put her in a room with a typical surround-sound setup, she could tell there were audio channels missing and that certain sounds were missing from different speakers. This allowed her to perfect the sound across the board for the home setup and improve the game experience, which up until that moment she thought was perfectly fine as it had worked on the setup she regularly worked on.

I will be honest—some of the best playtests I have ever had with the most amount of joy have been in a real-world experience, sitting on a couch with my workmates, trash-talking each other, laughing and being the players we are at home. It's a wonderful chance to get back to basics and enjoy yourselves, all the while checking for what could be improved.

Steps to Success

- Come up with three locations where players play their games.
- Come up with three gameplay situations that are different from yours.
- Learn how other people play video games, as yours is not the only way to play. The more you learn from others, the better you can help perfect the experience.

BETA: HERDING CATS

The Point

Not only do you need to stay on point with playing the game, you also need to help everyone else keep playing the game … kind of like herding cats to the finish line. Have you ever tried this? As a practice it's complete lunacy, but screw it—learn to be crazy.

Further Definition

Nearing the end of the project, everyone is desperately sick of the game, coupled with a deep-seated desire to have the thing done with and never see it again. It's at this time you should be there to keep everyone focused on the end goal, no matter what level of designer you are. I use the term "herding cats," which if you have ever tried is next to impossible unless you put food down in the location you want them to go toward after not feeding them for a while. The same theory applies for developers at the end of a project cycle. They need some form of incentive to keep their eyes on the game screen and not roam the web aimlessly for the latest movie trailer.

It's also in periods like this that the great temptation to focus on other things takes hold. Remember that whatever level of designer you are, you need to set a great example. To accomplish this, I suggest starting up a variety of competitions to keep everyone focused. Anything from internal leader boards to see who on the staff is the very best at the game to a beard-growing competition to see who can grow the craziest beard by final—offering a trophy as the reward (trophy stores can be found online and will make you one for any purpose). Little silly games and celebrations are really what galvanize a team together by the end and help keep their happiness levels up under trying and stressful times. Many fine team members have stayed late testing and playing the game to make sure they could beat someone they challenged the next day—and in the process felt a sense of satisfaction to be focusing on the product for their own personal goals. I personally used to task out each of my designers to come up with a few solutions to this problem every beta, and they always came up with hilarious things to help everyone finish the game with a smile on their face. As long as the focus is still on the product or related to it, you have succeeded in herding the cats.

Steps to Success

- Think up at least three competitions that can be easily done during the beta to final period and what silly prizes can be rewarded to the champions. (I once gave a prize of a tacky pineapple plate that people fought to keep on their desks for months to prove they were the best.)
- Think up three things you can do to help keep the team in good spirits, from lunchtime movies to a box of doughnuts in the morning.
- Learn to gauge the mood of the team and if it begins to waiver pull out something fun to help everyone finish strong—but remember to consult others first, as you're not the only one out there coming up with great ways to improve team health.

BETA: RELAX—IT'S IN EVERYONE'S BEST INTEREST

The Point

Take a deep breath and let it out. No matter how crazy everything is, you need to relax.

Further Definition

It's a lot easier for me to say to you, "Hey, just relax" than for you to do it. On many occasions in a development of a game, you are the opposite of relaxed and feel the pressure to complete the product like a gun at the back of your head. This means you need to set up support structures to remind yourself to relax or you'll end up a stress case and destroy yourself as well as your team.

What each of us can do to relax is a matter of personal preference, but what I have seen work with many people is setting relaxation goals to remind yourself that no matter what is going on you can handle it with a relaxed, clear head. These goals can be as simple as stopping to take a deep breath every time you enter or exit a room, or spending thirty minutes a day walking outside. What makes you relax is specific to you—I'm just reminding you to figure out some small actions to do daily that support you. Through repetition and focus, they can become positive daily habits.

When you're relaxed, you tend to listen more than speak, you let annoyances fall from you without them affecting you, and you realize that stress holds you back from getting things done. Now, don't get me wrong—a sense of urgency and a deadline can be positive stress to make sure you are pushing yourself to get the job done by a certain point. I'm just letting you know that succumbing to stress is a killer (literally) and will destroy you along with your life.

I worked with a designer who would be overwhelmed by his stress but only a week before a milestone was about to hit. Like a light switch turned on, he would become stressed about everything from the littlest feature to the largest play-through experience. Worst of all, his emotional outbursts would tire out the team, who would have to expend energy to calm him down instead of getting the milestone done. This went on for years, and he was shown his actions as being negative almost every time. Somehow, he just couldn't change, so his managers just learned to expect it when a milestone was about to hit, with them setting up safer situations where his effect would be felt the least. He never seemed to get ahead in his profession, as no one could agree that he could handle stress well. He finally changed this pattern by asking a fellow developer to send him a text whenever he was going off the rails to help him understand what to do to get back on track. It worked like a charm, and I watched him stop midsentence in a rant when he heard the text message sound from his phone. This went on for a year, and in the end he wasn't debilitated by his stress anymore. He had worked hard and conquered it.

Steps to Success

- Take a deep breath and relax your shoulders. DO IT. I'll wait.
- Take more deep breaths every day. Consciously do this five times daily.
- Set up a relaxation system and do it over the next week.

BETA: PREPARE YOURSELF FOR INTERVIEWS

The Point

As you have been perfecting yourself into the lean, mean, you know everything about the game machine, you will have to prepare for the possibility that you might be asked to speak about it to the media. Being the person who knows the game best can force you to introduce it to those who don't know it.

Further Definition

If you have the gift of the gab and the knowledge of the game, you will inevitably be put in front of the camera or asked to write answers to questions from the media. This should be taken in the same vein as everything else in design—a solution waiting to happen. Take it from me, a great interview can help the sales of your game exponentially.

After an interview is out, the online community will discuss it endlessly in forums, so there are a few things to remember. First, you have to look the part, which means getting a haircut, wearing clothing styled for that medium of entertainment yet still you, and keeping yourself in a state of decent fitness. Don't be the greasy overweight human wearing a threadbare geeky T-shirt. That's how we get stereotyped, people. If you're going to sell someone on your game, you need to look the part of a professional. Second, you need to practice your delivery of information. Get everyone around you to do mock interviews and grade your performance. It will hurt, but as with everything, practice makes perfect. Third, you need to be able to deliver smooth, intelligent lines about the game that leave the interviewer asking follow-up questions rather than you blithering on endlessly about minor features no one cares about. Fourth, you need to be able to talk about your major feature set not from a design perspective but from a marketing one where the sell is the main focus. Finally, look happy and be excited about your product. Show the world they will be missing out on that happiness if they don't play your game. This point cannot be stressed enough—you are the ambassador to the world for your game, and you need to be able to speak accurately about it with passion.

A great interview can quite literally equate to preorder sales, as it's seen by a massive section of the populace that might not have normally cared about your product, and they might put in a preorder as soon as your interview airs. If you're entertaining in a unique way, you can also become a focal point for the game that the game-buying populace might connect with, turning you into Mr. or Ms. "Insert Game Name Here." Just remember you are the evangelist, not the religion, and you will do fine. Practice, practice, practice!

Steps to Success

- Go treat yourself to new outfit and a haircut to look your best.
- Get friends or coworkers to help you practice by running you through mock interviews and have them grade your performance.
- Take what you have learned and practice it until you're amazing.

BETA: LOVE QA EVEN MORE

The Point

You have to adore the job that QA is doing for the game and remember to treat them with respect. Avoid the unnatural desire to hunt them for sport in a deserted manor house on a desolate rain-swept island, even when you really want to.

Further Definition

By the bitter end, the QA team members are not your friends. They are a group of flying monkeys sent from some unholy evil genius to stop your game from getting out the door by finding more bugs. You have a life to lead, you're sick to death of looking at the same thing, and you fall asleep every night wishing this was all over. Over the years, my subconscious has created a recurring dream of getting the final approval email, crawling under my desk with a bottle, and drinking to forget the entire experience ever happened. Say what you will about my mind, this is a well-developed dream that includes my need for success, contemplation of what has happened throughout the project, and celebration at the end of it—which only comes when QA says I can have it. With that being said, during beta you need to put all of your personal crap aside and love QA that much more (evil flying monkeys need love too … I checked). These people are the backbone of the cycle at the very end, and I can't even count the late nights I have stood beside them trying to find the game-stopping bug or verifying a fix with them into the wee hours of the morning. Over my time in gaming, I have dealt with more QA people than I can put names to faces (sorry to anyone I have worked with when you wave at me and I look right through you—I'm really bad at remembering faces). I truly respect the ones who bring me the dreaded news at zero hour, because they care.

My personal favorite was a guy I used to offer a beer to every time he came up with a show-stopping bug. I swear for a good two weeks I kept that kid in booze every night, and he went home happy that he was doing a great job to boot. I could tell he cared and that the smallest offering I could give back to him would be appreciated as we both wanted the same thing: a high-quality game out on the market. As hard as it is, QA is still focused on a top-quality product and you need to respect them for that, even as you shake your fist in disgust when they bring you yet another show-stopper that keeps you from making final for yet another day.

Steps to Success

- Work closely with your QA team at the end and be there the moment they find something to stop shipping the game.
- Offer up incentives in any form to keep them hunting for the bug that no one thought was there. Given any incentive, you will see, they will yield amazing results.
- Respect them even when they are at the bottom of the totem pole. You never know—one might be on your team as a designer one day or as your manager (don't laugh, I've seen it happen). Respect all levels of staff.

CHAPTER 7

Final

CONTENTS

Level 7: Final 164
Final Definition 166
Final: Chart Your Shipped Bugs 168
Final: Give Up on Praise 169
Final: Dust Off Your Blue Sky Notes 170
Final: Do a Postmortem 172
Final: Celebrate Your Victories 173

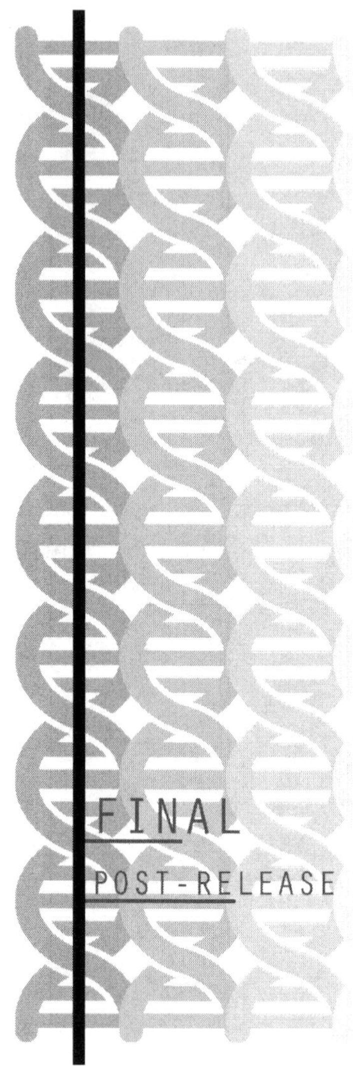

LEVEL 7: FINAL

This is it, the final level you have heard so much about from all the way back to the beginning of the game as a mythical place that developers speak of in hushed circles imbibing countless fermented vegetable drinks. Once you walk into these sacred grounds you know you're in a special place of reverence, but nothing prepares you for the final beast of evil, the beast known as First Party. This is the final boss, and if the game's level progression has taught you anything, it's going to be a doozy. You're ready for this, you keep telling yourself like some form of ancient mantra that will make everything better, but deep down you know that this is the final test and there is no failing this one. There is only pass, win, go to the end.

By this point in the development cycle, you more or less have become the master of all worlds you have dealt with. This mastery is across the depth and breadth of the game having spent many hours on every part—if you did it right, of course. You have melded all worlds into you and gained all that they have as a part of you. This incorporation of power, knowledge, and experience has brought you the ability to smell a bug at 30 paces. You have become the end all, be all of the game, and you are now the one your allies come to when they don't know how to eradicate any bug monster. It's at this point that you realize it's no longer just about destroying individual bugs. You have reached the understanding that you are now the venerable one who others seek out to learn how to kill the bugs themselves. You're the teacher, the scholar, and on your best days a little bit of a deity walking around the level like you already know what's going to happen before it occurs. In your most arrogant of moments, you move without even opening your eyes and realize this is what Neo must have felt like.

As you come to the final field of battle, your allies by your side as grizzled veterans, you know it's finally time to fight the last great battle. Yet this battle is far more difficult and different from anything you have ever faced. First off, you will present your record of accomplishments from the entire game, and then a shadow group vaguely resembling your own ally judges will appear to evaluate you for the third time. By this point you're really sick of being judged, but take heart, it will be over soon. Bugs appear in lands you swear were bug-free levels, and when you're not looking these foul and detestable judges will dream up a few bugs you didn't know even existed. After you have dealt with all of the issues on their lists and haggled over the ones that you know no one will ever see, the head judge will give you a pass or fail. Like alpha and beta, this can happen many times until you finally get the pass you're looking for. When that happens, they will bestow upon you the final part of the robot you have been dragging around since the alpha level. This is the moment you have been waiting for, and you busily assemble the robot for launch. The robot spins up its power core and with a salute fires off into the sky, launching itself out to the wide world you have never seen. As it arcs in the sky, a small single tear drips down your face, as you know you have done something impossible and that makes you mighty. FIN, roll credits, fade to black.

FINAL DEFINITION

The Point

The sixth period of a games cycle is called Final where everything is wrapped up to ship it off.

Further Definition

SWEET UNDEAD ZOMBIE ATTACK! IT'S OVER! During final, designers are really on call to give answers to anything and around to continue testing anything that comes back from first party (first party is the platform your game is going out on). Final can happen in a lot of different ways because the final build is not always the final build that gets shipped off. If you're dealing with a platform, they have their own quality assurance testing that they go through before it can be manufactured. On PC, it's really up to the developer/production company much of the time. That means a new host of bugs from major to minor can arrive, and the developer needs to decide what they are going to fix to satisfy the platform's requirements or what bugs they can ship with reasonable answers back to first party. This back and forth process can cause games to miss ship dates, deal with bugs they didn't want to touch, and require more final builds than anyone wants to admit (now serving 73 … would final build 73 please stand up). All of these occurrences are dirty little secrets that users and reviewers don't see, yet this is the real world of video games development. The best course of action with this is to just offer up all of your knowledge to the production team so that they can make the best decisions. It's their responsibility, and the best you can do is aid them where you can. If and when you find out your game has finally jumped through all of the hoops needed, you have reached final, at which point you can fall over. (Literally, people actually just fall over. I've seen it, so provide soft pillows wherever you think it might happen.)

A few times a game I have been working on has gone straight from beta to final to ship in one day, which means you should be prepared for any eventuality. Be the ninja who knows what to do when your assassination job has gone south and then act on that solution. I personally relish with great intensity the email communication from production that the game has shipped, having been known to leap from my chair and run through the office screaming, "WOOO HOOO IT'S ALL OVER!" followed by much celebration.

Steps to Success

- Be present and there to offer any information you can to help out production. Think of yourself as the dark advisor behind the king's throne who fills their ear with the right way to run the kingdom.
- Do not get discouraged by multiple final builds. It's actually very normal and a great learning exercise if you choose to see it that way.
- When all is said and done, remember to celebrate your achievement. What you have made brings a little piece of light to a dark universe.

FINAL: CHART YOUR SHIPPED BUGS

The Point

When you have a second to breathe, make a list of the bugs that made it into the game that you would really like to be dealt with. You never know how handy that list might be.

Further Definition

Every single product has shipped bugs. It's something that is a necessity to finishing the game by the dates set out. If there was all the time in the world, then everything would get sorted, but since that happens like 0.01% of the time, expect the shipped bugs folder to be big.

At the end of a project it's a really good exercise to collect all of the shipped bugs together and grade them according to their levels of ugliness from your point of view. As a designer, you have a unique perspective on what the end user is looking for and what they would enjoy seeing in the end product. I'm sorry to say it, but a tiny discolored polygon on a faraway hilltop in level 72 when viewed from a certain vantage point does not particularly count in your top ten list of bugs to fix if given the chance. Gathering the shipped bugs will give you a great perspective on what exactly was missing from the final game when viewed by themselves. From there, select a short list of bugs and figure out with each of the disciplines what it would take to fix them by having some lighthearted discussions about them. When you have all of your ducks in a row, present your findings to production or your team lead. This is good for a couple of reasons, because you never know what is going to happen in the long run. The game could need a patch, in which case these bug fixes might be slipped in. The game could get some add-on content or the game might be a yearly iteration title, in which case these should be the first bugs that development starts fixing for the next version. On a few wondrous occasions the dates for my game had been pushed out, and the list I had generated became the first-fix list for the production team because I had presented it to them with reasoning why these bugs should be fixed first. If you get into the habit of doing this, it will help out the production team a lot and push the issues you want fixed to the forefront before everyone else gets their muddy little gips on them. (That's right, engineering, I see you over there looking at me with your shipped-issue list.) The point is to be the person to think about this first and show you're looking to the future rather than falling over the moment everything is done. This shows everyone your dedication to the product's success (psst, your career's success too).

Steps to Success

- Find all of the shipped bugs for the product and review them in the game.
- Group the shipped bugs into categories from "would be nice to fix" to "I really don't care."
- Take the top 25% of the issues you believe should be dealt with and make a list that you send to production to keep in their back pockets. Back-pocket lists are a designer's bread and butter.

FINAL: GIVE UP ON PRAISE

The Point

A designer's job is a thankless one, and even if you get praise it's normally offset against a massive amount of Internet criticism.

Further Definition

Fundamentally, you might want everyone in the wide world to adore your work and focus yourself around trying to get that. I'm here to tell you, it doesn't work that way. No matter how hard you try, your work will be misunderstood by many, from fellow developers to the general player audience. Reviewers and fellow developers might praise your back-of-the-box feature set (that's your big features for the game), but many will neglect the finer points unless they are annoyed by them.

I've worked with a designer who spent a year straight tuning guns for a shooter game from damage to spray pattern along with everything in between. The moment the guns were present in the game, production only complained about them and never gave him any positive feedback. Over time, he realized that "positive feedback" was when they stopped giving feedback on a specific gun and moved on to the next one. As the game evolved, the production staff went back and started the whole list again before the game shipped. When the game came out, the player base did the same thing and specifically chewed apart every call the team had made, which he in turn fixed in a patch post-launch as well as a subsequent DLC. After a year of only hearing negative feedback about what he had spent his work life perfecting, for his sanity he asked to be moved off guns and focused on another area. The management obliged as they had seen the beating he had taken—no other designer had gotten the amount of feedback he had. In the end he told me, "I just want to do something people like or don't care about."

One of the best quotes I heard from a beloved manager sums this up to a T: "The best you can hope for is that no one noticed you." That means you didn't screw up, which causes untold amounts of criticism, and you got the job done right. Silence is your praise and should be taken as such. It sounds odd, but it requires you to bestow your own praise on yourself and stop needing external validation to remind you that you're doing a great job. That's not to say that you might not be lauded with praise for a great game, but that's a rare occurrence.

As an example, I wrote this book to help people in game design, not to be thanked for it. My reward was writing it, finishing it, and getting it published for me as a personal goal. To that end I rewarded myself with positive praise every step of the way to remind me I can do mighty things and that I am the one who I should want the most praise from.

Steps to Success

- Openly praise yourself today for who you are. Life is hard, so be easy on yourself.
- Do a good deed for a friend without expectation of praise. Just help.
- Select any game and read up on all the user reviews from great to horrible. Imagine you designed it and how you would feel after.

FINAL: DUST OFF YOUR BLUE SKY NOTES

The Point

Remember that Blue Sky list I had you keep in your drafts folder? Well, now is finally the time to blow off the dust that has been collecting on it and see what you have generated throughout the whole adventure.

Further Definition

Now that you are done with the project, it's finally time for that Blue Sky email I got you to create and find out what everyone else did. Think of it as a convenient time capsule you get to open up as the project's ending. You might surprise yourself and others about what you came up with keeping this log, and really, that's the point, as this list is a complete shoulda woulda coulda document. Many times I'm personally shocked what my sleep-deprived brain has gotten me to document when my cognitive thinking wasn't working. Of course a racing game needs flying babies on the fifth level to pull the narrative together ... gah. Not all Blue Sky thoughts are great, but there are always kernels of greatness.

When you have finished patting yourself on the back or being shocked what you thought was worthy to put down on the page, organize a meeting with all of the design team to sit down in front of a whiteboard and detail everything you have generated. Spend the time to break it up into major/minor categories that could help make the game greater. Discuss with everyone the pros and cons to every single point, then get them to choose five major ones in a blind vote along with five minor ones. From that list figure out what the top five are for each group and pass one out to each designer to write up a short explanation about. The explanation can be really very simple—just a one-pager to get the core of the idea across. Add in some visuals as well to spice up the document, as that always helps the sell. Remember that unlike core design this list will be going to production and should be written for them as a kind of sell sheet. When everyone is done, collect all of the data together and send it out to the production team as a wish list document for the future. The simple act of keeping a running Blue Sky list will put you head and shoulders above the rest, and organizing the meeting shows you care about the game's continued success. I have seen this unrequested list I generated with design used in a meeting the day after it was sent to solidify a contract for an add-on pack generating the company continued work for the year. That really wasn't the point of it originally, but as it was there it was something to dazzle the production house into forking out more cash to the developer for the future work. You would be pleasantly surprised how this document gets used quite a bit by many members of staff for everything from patches to add-ons to a possible next title.

Steps to Success

- Dust off your Blue Sky list and have a meeting about it with designers.
- Get every point in a major/minor list on a whiteboard to vote on.
- Get everyone to write one page on each point, collect them all, and send it to production.

FINAL: DO A POSTMORTEM

The Point

At the end of every project, you as well as the team should do a postmortem on what worked or didn't during the game's life cycle. I call this the butcher's bill.

Further Definition

Doing a postmortem is something everyone in games should do. Whether it comes to actual use is a different story. What that means is that you have to want to grow from your mistakes and the mistakes of the group for the future. You and the team are not perfect. Many times the group isn't interested in that type of growth because it worked in the end and no matter what happened it all sorted itself out. To them, the ends justify the means, which guarantees making the same mistakes again. That's garbage, and after years of seeing postmortems disappear into oubliette folders never to be seen again, I'm here to say you personally should do them for your own growth. Even if it hurts and there is a boatload of improvement needed, it has to be done.

That said, make one up for you and your department on an anonymous poll website that everyone helps create. Spend some quality time going back to think about what you did well and didn't do well (it's hard, I know, but hey, so is life, which is filled with mistakes). It's a lot easier to break it up into three levels, such as what was amazing, what was passable, and what can be improved on. This will let you know how to categorize items and keep things focused rather than an unorganized bitch session which postmorts can turn into. Fill it in about yourself and your team without any emotional bias (almost impossible, I know, but you need to be dispassionate sometimes to help everyone improve). Then collect all of the data into a report to send off to your managers.

Now, here is the hard part. You now need to actually take what you and your department have done poorly and fix it. Easy to say, but you would be floored how many times no one is willing to do this, which is why these reports somehow end up in the river with cement shoes. More often than not, it has to do with what I call a literal truth, which is when everyone knows it's a problem, it involves people above their pay grade, and those people aren't going to change their ways, making the statement of truth in a postmortem a useless waste of time that could be career threatening. Sad, I know all too well, so the best you can hope for is do it for yourself, as you are responsible for your own success. If nothing else comes of the feedback it will be a great asset for your manager to help you grow as a developer, and they will respect you for being self-aware of your own faults coupled with the desire to improve.

Steps to Success

- Use a template you have devised to give yourself a postmortem.
- Get others in your department to do it too about every topic they can think of.
- Finally, work at making the ugly parts better no matter how much it hurts.

FINAL: CELEBRATE YOUR VICTORIES

The Point

When the game has gone final, you need to remember that you have helped finish it and that a massive undertaking has been accomplished, which means you need to celebrate yourself for a job well done. No matter how you feel about the final product going to market, it's an achievement.

Further Definition

When I finished my first game and I got the email that it would be out in the world, I remember falling out of my chair, going into the fetal position, then crawling under my desk to sleep. No joke. Sleep for me on that project was my celebration, and as the years have gone by it still is, as having the ability to sleep in on a given day is a glorious thing. I realized really early on that so many people on a team just didn't celebrate the game being done when it actually happens, suspending themselves to wait for the returns on the sales numbers and the review scores. These are dangerous points to focus on, as developers can be completely crushed by sales and review scores. Personally as an artisan this never sat well with me because the act of creation and completion were both monumental and deserving of celebration. To counter this, I always have an email to the entire team ready to send the moment I hear the game is done, detailing all of the great things people have done to make sure the game was completed. Think of that mail like a thank-you speech when winning an award (I'd like to thank ...). It's an important skill to celebrate the moments you have, because tomorrow you might be on another game or doing something completely different. Those tiny moments of success need to be blown up to a massive level to remind you that the whole team is a success. The little token reminds everyone—even if they are not in any mood to care—that they have been amazing to help finish the product and should be recognized for it. After I've sent this mail, I have had hardened developers come to my desk in tears because they had forgotten that they were great and that makes them mighty.

On many occasions, everyone is too busy thinking of their base needs (i.e., sleep) and forget even the simplest act of saying "job well done" to themselves. If you ever forget to do this, you have lost the passion to make games, and I kindly ask that you exit the industry by whatever door you happen to kick yourself out of. Celebrate your wins, as one's life is not always filled with them.

Steps to Success

- Write down all of the great things people do throughout the project. Then mail it to your team or company when the game is done.
- Celebrate by whatever means you require to remind yourself you have just done a great thing.
- Buy yourself a meaningful gift to commemorate your accomplishment so that every time you see it you're reminded YOU ROCK! Because you do.

CHAPTER 8

Post-release

CONTENTS

Level 8: Post-release 176
Post-release Definition 178
Post-release: It's Alive, Kill It Now! 180
Post-release: Patch Plan—Have One 181
Post-release: Visit Your Product in the Stores 182
Post-release: Review Scores and Bottom Line 184
Post-release: Put It on the Wall 185
Post-release: Nothing to Do Is a State of Mind 186
Post-release: Be Working on Something Already 188
Post-release: What Happens When You Win 189

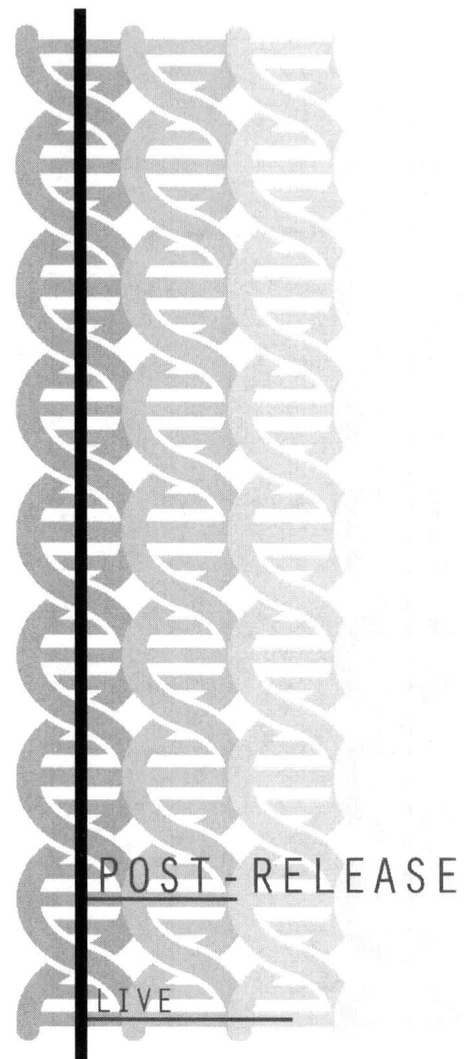

LEVEL 8: POST-RELEASE

Hold up—you thought it's all over. You saw credits, and FIN means finish, right? Is this some trick of the post-credits scene you didn't know about? The game is done, it's out in the world, and now you can rest knowing that you did the job justice. At least, that's what you thought as you now have a front-row seat to watch your robot fly through the cosmos. It's on its own trajectory, it's on a mission now.

You now have little to no control of what will happen to your precious robot flying around the stars. Through your actions that built this little bit of technology, it's going to have to fight its own battles with the venerable Players Consortium and the feared Reviewer Empire. Both can all but destroy your robot in front of your eyes. It's overwhelmingly painful to be this powerless after being in control of the game itself, but this is the part no one ever talks about and you're now forced to watch all of your decisions be analyzed by people you have never met. The only thing to keep you from going mad is that most robots will let you know if they have succeeded in the first two weeks after launch.

The only allies you can call on to help your robot succeed take the form of the often background and sparingly used marketing and social media warriors. Both of these allies normally don't have the heavy lifting to contend with until the launch has happened, and then it's all about what they can do to help that robot fly even higher against every adversary. They can be the difference between a platinum robot soaring the skies all ablaze with wonderment and a junker that exploded, killing dozens of hapless bystanders with shrapnel flying back to hit you in the face.

Added to this you will have to go back to all of the levels and clean up all of the bug monsters you didn't have time to crush on the way to the end as there was a clock over your head the whole time. Even though your passion for doing this is at an all-time low, there is a part of you that is a completionist that needs to clean them all out. All this is in an effort to add a few extra parts to your spacefaring robot, as that's now your main concern. This is the time when all the major battles are done, but you can't let go as there are a few smaller ones left.

This is also the moment where you have the freedom to live. Just live, just be, and you choose what needs to be done rather than what you are required to do. It's like you were on a track the whole time, so busy to get to the end that when it's all done you're left with only memories. It's the time to put your shield down, remembering all the battles it helped you survive, take your armor off, not forgetting to inspect it for the last time for all the battle damage, and place your sword on the mantle to remind you what you fought for, as you will never get that experience back again. Now that the adventure is done, you can walk out into the sunshine, smile, and know you did your best. No matter what your robot does now, it's out of your hands, and the best you can do is prepare for the next game if you're lucky enough to be a part of one. And so love goes and so life goes and so you go. You carry on.

POST-RELEASE DEFINITION

The Point

The game is now completed, and you should take some time to rest, evaluate, and look to the future. It's not just about falling over it's more about understanding what's next as there is always more work to do and from the launch of the game to the end of the first month is the post-release period you'll do it in.

Further Definition

During this period, the designer is really at their lowest productivity level and the office looks like a ghost town after a ghostbuster has been through. You would think that your job is done, but truth be told it's never really done until you're actually working on the next game or patch. (Patching is one or more fixes that will be applied to the game in an update.) When you're on another game, that's when you can actually say it's finally done. In this period, your game will be sold on the market, sales figures will start coming in, and review scores will start appearing in all forms of media. Breathe deep and let it be okay. It's hard—no one ever prepares you for the sales figures and what reviewers will say about the game you have lived with for so long. (Insert ancient curse on all reviewers here.)

You have to prepare for when your game comes out late after its marketing, misses all of its set sales forecasts, and gets reviewed as the biggest waste of time that year. Every criticism will hurt and force you to go to a very dark place questioning yourself about every decision you have made for the project. It's good to question oneself but don't fall into the Möbius strip of beating yourself up about it. You made your calls and have to live with them no matter the end result. Take solace in that and know that you did your best. Your art is out there, and as much as you feel you would like to go up and fix it at the gallery opening, it just can't happen that way. It's no surprise that your happiness is directly tied to the success of the product as you have put so much of yourself into it. Disassociate yourself from the product. Learn to think of it like it's a child, not an appendage. You do your best to prepare a child for this world, yet they will do what they will, while an appendage is a part of you and you're directly responsible for its actions.

The best advice I can give is that missed dates happen, the market is fickle for sales with no magic formula for success, and reviews are just a state of perception from that person on that day. You're better than all of this, and I sincerely hope your product goes platinum and you continue making games far into the future. Whatever you do, avoid hunting down the reviewers no matter how much you want to. Be the better human.

Steps to Success

- Separate your emotional happiness from the success or failure of the game. Now say it out loud … and again until it sticks.
- Rest and recuperate because you might not get another chance, and you're useless to everyone if you're not in top form.
- Remember you're better than the moment you find yourself in, and you just created a video game … and that makes you mighty.

POST-RELEASE: IT'S ALIVE, KILL IT NOW!

The Point

No matter what you think you have covered, when a game is live something will come out of far-left field that you never expected, which will need to be dealt with in the most efficient way possible to keep players enjoying the game.

Further Definition

Issues will appear like those pesky moles in a whack-a-mole game, with your group's job to bash them down as fast as they come up. No matter what team size you worked with to develop your game, you never know what will happen to the code when hundreds to millions of people jump on the game at the same time. Think of the players as playtesters who paid for the privilege of showing you what's wrong with your game—except they always expect everything to be perfect, which no code ever is. This means you need to take the following steps to get some kind of handle on this chaotic period.

When a new critical issue is identified, just breathe. No, seriously, people throughout history have just stopped when chaos erupted around them and took a long, deep breath to center themselves. This helps to focus your mind and connect you with the chaos instead of letting it overwhelm you. Next, try to get as much information as you can about the issue. The Internet is famous for presenting a problem that is in fact a completely different issue. The more information you have, the better you can work with your team to architect a fix—and yes, you need to architect the fix out before you build anything as it will be connected to a great many areas. Next work, closely with the group making the fix, offering your services as a live-in QA member to verify it before QA sees it. (QA has its place, but as very few critical issues come in during this period typically, it's possible to be there to check them out first). Once the fix is solid, QA will test the living bejesus out of it from every angle, and a release date can be set for the fix in communication with the first-party provider.

Believe me when I say players don't want to have to update with dozens of hotfixes to play the game—one collected for that day is generally tolerable. That said, a critical crash bug that stops players playing needs a fix rushed out to unblock players who can't get the game finished. Learn to fix fast, solid, and be prepared to monitor the fix when it goes live to players to chart the fix's success.

Steps to Success

- Breathe, and practice breathing regularly as the world could use people taking a deep breath instead of reacting emotionally.
- Offer your services to everyone who needs it. Lose your ego—if they need something, offer it up to support them.
- Once the fix is out in the world you need to track how it's being taken. If possible, work with your marketing people to communicate out what the fix is and when it's set for release. Players calm down when they know a fix is coming.

POST-RELEASE: PATCH PLAN—HAVE ONE

The Point

Most games with a reasonably sized team will work out a patch schedule for delivering features/fixes for your game. If they don't, you should be the one to present them with one, as patches will last from post-release into LIVE.

Further Definition

This logic follows along the lines of he who is first, WINS. This means that if there is no plan for a patch or features set out to add to the game to make it better, you should be the first one to make that list. You need to have the pulse of the nasty bugs that are hindering the product and the features will best wow the players.

Patches by nature take on two forms: hotfix and planned. Hotfixes I've explained already and are mostly emergencies. Planned, on the other hand, is where I suggest you put in your efforts. All of this said, patches normally follow this schedule: Day 0, Day 1, Day 7, Day 14, Day 30, Day 60, and Day 90. (Note: Mobile will have a much faster patch schedule.) All of these are points on or past the release of the game, to keep it all in perspective. To get a plan together, I break this down to a formula, as follows: Time/Working Days × Amount of Staff = Total Work Number. Then take your list of bugs and get an estimate on the fix time from the staff you work with. Bugs can be in increments of .25 (2 hours), .5 (4 hours), and 1 (a full work day.) See what fits into the patch Total Work Number, with your own stack ranking from most desired to least.

If the bugs you want fixed fit into the Total Work Number you have, then that is your patch. If there happens to be too many, then you have to make a cut list of bugs that won't make it for that patch, which will become the next ones to fix for the following patch. Day 0, Day 1, Day 7, and Day 14 patches are mostly for bug fixes, stabilization, and performance improvements. For Day 30, Day 60, and Day 90 patches, add in the variable for features. For features, follow the same logic and figure out from your list how long features will take to complete, accounting for test time to fully complete them (features typically follow the system of 1, 3, 5, 7, 10 days to complete for estimates). Then follow the same system as with the bugs and see what will make it onto a features list. This gives you two lists to work with, both applied against the Total Work Number. Now, for the final step, make the call of which has more value to do in the time given, features vs. bugs. A mix of both is best and with a selection of top priority work items you can get to the Total Work Number.

Steps to Success

- Make a list of bugs and features you want fixed.
- Make your own formula based off mine and make up a patch plan.
- Be the first to build this out and deliver it to the powers that be, as it more than helps put forth the areas you want the company to focus on for the game's benefit.

POST-RELEASE: VISIT YOUR PRODUCT IN THE STORES

The Point

When your game is released in retailer or online, spend the time to go and see it. Seeing is believing and that makes it real.

Further Definition

This part follows along the lines of celebrating achievements and is something I have watched disappear in the industry, which is sad to say. The game released is a symbol of your team's success in making something that the public is going to buy and enjoy. The whole point of the exercise of making a game is to complete it, and seeing it is the completion point. That symbol is a very powerful reminder that anything, even when it's perceived to be impossible, can be achieved. Take a moment and pat yourself on the back for a job well done. Remember all of the times you spent putting everything together with the entire team and the countless hours you spent glued to the screen making the game better. I'm a fan of the personal high five and I don't care who sees me doing it. I like to remind myself I rock, as most people never will, which isn't a bad thing as you have to know yourself that you have succeeded. Remember that the game took a decent portion of your life to finish and took all your passion to complete.

The trip to the shop is kind of like the final piece of the puzzle you have been working on since the idea was mentioned to you when the project started. Now it's done and no one can say any different. I myself make a pilgrimage to the shops to see my products the day they are released and spend a good few minutes in awe that it's happened again with the anti-hero living at the end to tell the tale. Hell, I even get my picture taken with it and post it on whatever social networking sites I care about to announce to the electronic world that I win. That's right, big old world, I have created something and I am proud of it. Now say that three times and you will start to understand the feeling.

I hope that everyone gets the chance to do this and feel a sense of success because it's needed. I also suggest that you do it before it drops off the games radar and you find your success in the bargain bin. That always hurts inside every time I see it, even though it's a reality in entertainment media. It's still a little stab to the chest cavity that your success is currently in the must-go bin at the local retailer or reduced in price online. Basically it's just best to perform the ritual on the day of release and make a celebration out of it. You'll thank me later.

Steps to Success

- Go to the shops or online on the day of your game's release.
- Actually think about the entire experience and what it's meant to you. Introspection is good for the soul, done sparingly.
- Take at least one photo of you holding the game and promptly stick it on a social networking site for everyone to see. You WIN!

POST-RELEASE: REVIEW SCORES AND BOTTOM LINE

The Point

Review scores and the games sales figures are what run the games industry. It's a business and you need to treat it like that, a business. Cold and unemotional.

Further Definition

As much as everyone has an opinion on what is a great game, the real way to tell if a game is a good one is checking the total review scores and how much it actually sold.

I have a little story that illustrates this from my own personal history. When I started as a designer, my executive producer told me that I would be judged largely on three things: if my game made its dates, a high total review score, and if it made its sales targets. For the first few projects, I lived by this and got pretty much every one of those covered with every game I did. Then one year I got tossed a project that the company needed to handle due to contractual issues and had 40% of the time needed to make it properly. I did get it out the door on time (design gods, forgive me for that butt-ugly baby), and when the review scores came back it was the lowest collective review score in that company's history. I was promptly taken into a meeting where I was told I had only one more game to make good or I would be fired. Instead of blaming them for tossing me that game they knew would fail, I fought for a better next game. After six weeks, a funny thing happened—a marketing person for the company contacted me to let me know that the game had sold 30% better than expected over the first month of release and I should pat myself on the back. I was dumbstruck, and the first thing I did was walk up to the executive producer to tell him the great news. It did not have the intended effect I was hoping for. Instead of being happy, he was annoyed at being showed up as wrong about the game, but he begrudgingly agreed to lift the dreaded black spot against me. I continued making great games under proper timelines that got great reviews … and the executive producer never forgave me for showing him up.

This story is to illustrate that dates need to be met for marketing to sell your game (they can also be moved slightly if the game is big enough to warrant it, which no one ever tells you until it happens), review scores are generally there for the company to show they make great games (review scores can and have been bought with marketing dollars), and the golden rule trumps everything because games is a business. Say it: games is a business and is there to make money.

Steps to Success

- Find out from your marketing/sales people how much the forecast is for your game and check up on the sales as much as you can.
- Check all of the review scores from all over the world, reading them with an open mind (props to Finnish reviewers!).
- Avoid the temptation to hunt down reviewers. They are just fallible people.

POST-RELEASE: PUT IT ON THE WALL

The Point

If your game has a physical unit, stick it into a frame and put it on the wall. It serves as a reminder that you have succeeded in making it. The symbol in physical form means something.

Further Definition

To make sense of this simple point, I think this fits into the category of you need to remember that you have had successes. If you put your game on the wall, you will see it daily and it will remind you that you can achieve great things. That is a piece of your life, your passion, and your time, which need to be respected. This is important as so few people keep their achievements with them in physical form, instead counting on their skewed memories to recall that period of their lives.

Many years ago, I was introduced to a marvelous developer who when I met him had already worked on a dozen games. He was a god to me when I first started, as finishing even one game seemed almost impossible. He had every one of his games in frames with little plaques underneath detailing each, with the dates of their beginning and their end, along with the position he held. As I was shiny new to the industry, I didn't know anyone could survive that long in games and marveled at each as they were set up around his office in sequence, like a timeline of his life. All of them looked perfect until I got to one with a disk in it that had been smashed and then glued back in. I asked him what that was all about, and he calmly said, "That was a bad project. I thought I needed to remember that." By the time I left his office I had noticed a few more in pieces and said nothing more, out of respect. Since that day I have done the same thing with my games and I suggest you do it too. Just like the trip to the shops on the first day, putting your game into a frame is another great symbol to show your respect for what's been done. It doesn't matter if it sucked and you barely survived the experience—you still survived the game and lived to keep creating more (in the bloody worst case, it's an entry on your résumé to get a job somewhere else). Everyone suffers with bad projects because most of the time we don't have a great choice in which ones we end up doing or how most ended up. Most of a designer's career is spent on other people's ideas that turn into games—it's just a reality. That means no matter what, when it's done, frame it, put it up, and if you need to smash it first to remember it was a bad project, so be it. It was still a success you survived.

Steps to Success

- Get a copy of your game, have it framed with your position along with its start and end dates. Then hang it at home or at work to remind you of that adventure.
- Hang it in a place where you will see it frequently rather than in a place you barely ever visit. It's good during the hard times to see your accomplishments.
- Smash it or keep it intact depending what your total experience of the game was, as this will tell others what it was truly like for you. This ritual is a good one to pass on to others too.

POST-RELEASE: NOTHING TO DO IS A STATE OF MIND

The Point

If there is nothing to do, you should be using that time to improve your skills. It's not hard, you just have to have the drive to learn more, no matter how much you want to fall over.

Further Definition

Another great thing to do during your downtime between projects is to learn more. We are never bored as designers—if you're bored, get out of the industry as the world is full of mystery. We as people only fall into laziness when we limit ourselves with crap stories that we cannot do this or that.

Pick up a book on any topic that you think will help you be a better designer. Sketch, paint, listen to music, and learn to use new tools you never thought you would have the time to play with. This is never discouraged in a company because you are working to make yourself better—and if anyone says different, tell them you're working to better your experience as a designer, at which they will quickly leave you in peace. I speak from experience on this.

I had a junior designer once who was very much obsessed with fight sequences. In his downtime, he spent hours watching and cutting up fight sequences from movies to use for his personal research. The problem was our design director kept coming by and seeing him watching movies. One day, the design director called him into his office, and when he came out he had a book to read on time management. He was dumbstruck because he believed he had very good time management skills, which anyone who had actually worked with him knew was true. I went to the design director and had a chat about why he had done this and found out that he thought the junior designer was slacking off all day by watching movies, even though there was little to no work to do until the next game was signed. After an eye-opening explanation, I took him over to the junior designer's desk and showed him the work he had done filtering something like 50 fight sequences into a video to show fighting evolution in media over the last 30 years to educate the other designers, which left the director speechless. The director promptly took the time management book off the designer's desk and slinked back to his office. The lesson here is to learn what you can when you can, but remember to let everyone else know what you're up to as they might not understand. The perception of what you are doing and what you're doing with it is very important.

Steps to Success

- Read a book on a design topic you never expected to read and learn everything about it. Then share what you have learned with others as everyone can benefit from learning.
- Learn a new tool you never thought you would have time to learn, and (like with this book) go through it with others, showing them what you have learned.
- Let everyone know what you're doing or you'll end up with a dry business book on time management, which no one EVER wants.

POST-RELEASE: BE WORKING ON SOMETHING ALREADY

The Point

If there is no patch work to keep you busy, learn to be like a magician who always has something up their sleeves ready at any moment to dazzle the crowd. A card, a dove, a sparkly new feature . . . .

Further Definition

After a project is completed, there is a certain amount of downtime before the next one starts, and this is precious time for you to work on something of your own. This is different from learning—this is about doing. Take this time as a gift and spend real hours working on an idea or a few for games that your company could do in the future.

Treat this exercise as a treasure, as not everyone gets it. If nothing else, it's a great chance to expand your portfolio with all of the groovy things you learned while making the last game. You will be amazed how much you have learned from one game that you can apply to new design. I personally can't stand downtime and find that I get into the most trouble when I don't have all cylinders running at full. Learn from me and use your time instead of driving yourself crazy, which in turn leads you to act out in the most ridiculous ways. I'm not as bad as I was when I started, but that's because I learned that burning bridges to light my way was not the way to live my life. I have scars to prove it.

Over time, I have learned to keep myself entertained even when there is really no quantifiable work to get done, and you will be shocked that this can happen more than companies like to admit. During these periods, I set myself a daily task of coming up with at least five ideas for games, from the outlandish to the mundane. Then I select one to work on for the next few days and expand it into a one- to three-page pitch document. While working on this I'm still coming up with five new ones per day. When I feel like I'm done, I get my other terminally bored designers to go over them for their feedback and start making another one. Think of it as an assembly line of design. This state of constant imagination has saved my brain more times than I can recall and puts me in my own personal goal-setting zone where I produce design at a feverous pace. Plus, if you're smart enough to come up with a game that uses an in-house engine you just might have the chance to make it happen—this has actually happened. You should try it, as you very literally have nothing to lose and everything to gain. Those who dare, win, so go try.

Steps to Success

- Come up with something that produces design in downtime and do it.
- Create at least five game ideas per day during downtime, pick your favorite, and write it up as a pitch document. Learn that you are the only limitation to creation, and the most insane ideas have turned into games. They all came from the same place—the brain of someone who thought, why not try it out?
- Learn to never stop creating and to finish what you started. No one wants to read a half-baked idea about a game you have only given the slightest attention to.

POST-RELEASE: WHAT HAPPENS WHEN YOU WIN

The Point

What do you do when your game succeeds, and all of your hard work is being snatched up by players who think it's wonderful? Don't screw it up, of course.

Further Definition

Most designers are normally not prepared for success with a game. They haven't set themselves up to handle it as they have lived with the building of the game for such a decent amount of time. I've known some wonderful designers achieve success and then do everything to ruin it for themselves. Now, I'm sure you're wondering, how would they mess up a perfectly wonderful situation? Well, it comes from the specter of ego that haunts every designer.

Most games (not all, but most) make all of their revenue in the first two weeks after release and then have a sharp decline with occasional blips in sales over time around additions to it. This means most companies know if they have a success or failure on their hands in a very short space of time. If the sales match or exceed the expected sales target, you have a hit. When you have a hit, everyone wants to know more, from the press to the players. Every scrap of information you give out is treasured and lauded over, which is dangerous as it can increase the size of one's ego.

I knew a great designer who worked on a game for three years. It was released to great fanfare and it sold through the roof. He went from someone who had all but been a social hermit to being someone everyone wanted to talk to. Press engagements, online playtests, written interviews became his new regular job. He began speaking with players online regularly, and his ego grew with every day. He started telling his team that he was the star who made all the calls, told people online way too much of his own personal views, which caused online trolls to start hunting him, and mistreated his friends as he now felt that he should be in a better class of people. All this of course was due to him not being prepared for success and treating the opportunity rather poorly. As the months went on, his team wanted to work with him less, players online had nothing but bile for him, and many of his friends were not returning his calls. What damage he did in three months he had to spend the next two years crawling out of. A hard lesson but a lesson that changed him for the better.

When you win, be gracious, act with humility, and treat everyone around you with even more respect, as they helped you get to the place where you succeeded. Be a good winner where you can be. It will mark you as a better person, which will attract the best of people to your side.

Steps to Success

- The next time you win a game with people, be gracious and thank them.
- The next time you win in life's game, treat someone (anyone) to a reward. They deserve it, and giving will make you all the better.
- Learn that winning is okay and that checking your ego at the door will do you great service and make you a better person.

CHAPTER 9

Live

CONTENTS

Level 9: Live 192
Live Definition 194
Live: You Fight for the Users 196
Live: Live Will School You 197
Live: Fix the Boat Before Making a New One 198
Live: From Trolls to Heroes 200
Live: A/B/C/D … Q Testing 201
Live: DLC for You and Me 202
Live: Workflow Waves 204

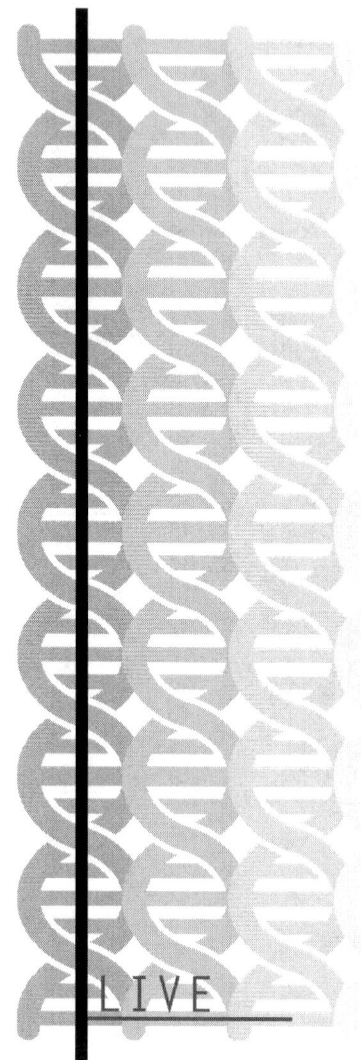

LEVEL 9: LIVE

Just when you thought you would never go back to the game, you suddenly are presented with a new set of missions in the same world you know all too well. They call these missions Downloadable Content and the Evergreen Experience. They revive your passion for the quest, and without a moment's question you suit up, hoist the shield, and pull the sword off the mantle where it's been collecting dust. It's time again for action, and you're not the type to refuse a call to action.

This new land is based on the previous levels you faced, but now there are two distinct areas. One is a bundle of experiences and another looks to be a boundless horizon that goes farther than your eyes can see. Both require your focus to build, as the Players Consortium has demanded more adventures for your robot, and you are nothing if not a shameless defender of the people's needs.

The bundled area will have you rushing again through all the levels you have already conquered (Levels 1 through 8) but this time in a massively smaller configuration. You think to yourself as you're rushing through the area that it's like the game got squished down to 10%, only showed off the greatest hits, and added a subplot narrative to keep you interested in the expedition. All the gates are there again with your impending sense of doom returning to hit you in the face when you least suspect it. Coupled with this, a new set of ordeals presents itself—yet they feel familiar when you slog through them, and that trip through the blackest of caves to meet the shadow doesn't scare you as much as it did the first time, as this one only has 10% of its potency. In the end, the bundled area will have its bug monster climax again, and a smaller group of allies will judge you a few times, bestowing an added robot part for you to fiddle with. If all goes well, your robot returns for its upgrade, and you go back to watching it from afar fly to new adventures across the cosmos, feeling a sense of completion. It's like you got the entire game experience again on fast-forward that deposits you back in your viewing chair safe and sound with that sword back up on the mantelpiece to again collect dust.

The other side of the level is the boundless horizon that to your eyes have smaller battles of bugs and missions that yield even tinier additions to your robot. The only difference is that this trek through the game—while manageable in comparison to the massive game quests themselves—seems to continue on forever. You add what you think is best for your robot and what the player consortium requests most of all over a spaced out period of time. Throughout this you carry on until you find the end of the level even if you cannot currently see it. One day this land and adventure too will end.

At the end of all things, the game is done, the further additions are done, and the boundless expanse will finish. As all things do. If they don't finish, how can they be judged for what they are, a work of art you helped create.

LIVE DEFINITION

The Point

The last period of a games cycle is called live, which is a state that a game lives in after it's launched. Live consists of monitoring, patching, and DLC that continue for as long as the game is popular. Please note that not all games have a live state, but most do to support their player base.

Further Definition

Well, now that your game's out into the world and being played you would think it would be the time for the designer to kick back with a Tiki drink as there is no wave to ride. You would be wrong. The live state of a game can mean the difference between continued sales over a long period and the bargain bin. Live can last for as little or as long as it's needed to support the game. Some games end live after one patch (patch is one or more fixes that will be applied to the game in an update) or fixing a few bugs, and some games have DLC/patch schedules that last years after launch. (DLC is downloadable content that will have new features, environments, and bugs.)

This means from the day it's live you need to be relentless in monitoring what is going on with your game to make sure there is nothing stopping players from enjoying their experience. If there are any issues, you need to patch them faster than you think is possible and get that out to players with the support of QA. Most of the time, though, fixes for the game are bundled into a patch that is scheduled for a certain period after the game launched (explained in chapter 8), which allows the team time to work out issues properly. DLC is a tricky thing as it's like a mini game really, which can be planned or unplanned. Planned DLC is when a company has worked out a deal to have it created over X amount of time which has marketing and hype around it. Unplanned DLC is when a game explodes and the fan base is amazing, which causes a DLC patch to be created. Truth be told, the planned is always better. The unplanned, while exciting, can become a hodgepodge of chaotic variables that don't always work out. The best thing for a designer to do is work with your team to prioritize what you can as important for a patch/DLC and work with them to get that done in the time you all have to complete it. Like the development cycle, this is a group effort and you need to understand that and work within that world.

Steps to Success

- Find out about your monitoring and watch the results like a hawk for any trends you start to find, as they can lead you to issues.
- Keep a level head when a critical bug comes in—a clear head in a crisis is worth dozens of headless chickens running around. Work with your team on a solid fix, test it as much as possible, and work with everyone for a hotfix release.
- Treat patches/DLCs as minor projects with development, alpha, and final periods in a much more condensed time period.

LIVE: YOU FIGHT FOR THE USERS

The Point

You need to fight for the player more than any other group and remember that you are in service of them instead of the other way around. Be the program that fights for the user.

Further Definition

To fight for the players, you need to do two things that sound easy yet are really very hard. You need to understand the player, and you need to be a ceaseless defender of what the player wants in the game. These actions are no easy feats when you will end up being about the farthest from a traditional player in thought and action, which means it's really hard to stand up for the player's needs. I didn't say it's impossible, just that it's hard as you're used to being the puppeteer rather than the puppet.

Most designers I know suffer from a god complex in some form or another—they have chosen to be the croupier instead of the gambler. Most designers will fight this for moral or religious reasons yet if those points are removed from the equation I have found they all have some form of the complex. If you ever have to ask if you have a god complex, just ask this simple question and really search yourself before answering: If you could be a god, would you? A designer at the heart of the game is a god that has determined the world, paths, progress, and hundreds of other variables that sum up to them that they are the gods of their particular little universe as it was designed by them. The problem comes when the god is asked to fight for the mortals, which involves putting themselves in the mortals' shoes. Thus, realizing you are probably not the best person to understand the player's mindset, you need to find other avenues to let their experience wash over you. This takes the form of watching silently as others play the game, only asking pointed questions occasionally about what they would like. Enter into forum conversations with players about what they would like to see added to the game. Many will literally give you a top ten list that's vetted and voted on as they feel ownership of the game. Needless to say, you need to come up with new ways to be the player so that you can learn from them.

Once you have figured out what the player wants (not what you want in the guise of the player), you need to put it on a banner, stick it in the ground, draw a sword and fight anyone who tries to stop you from delivering what the players want/need. (All metaphorically here, so please don't draw a real sword in your office.) If someone tries to circumvent this, show them the data behind your calls. Data always shuts down emotion, and 20 pages of forums demanding a feature tends to silence others in any meetings.

Steps to Success

- Figure out three unique ways to watch people play your game.
- Actually do at least one of the ways you created to view your players.
- Win a debate on features with fellow developers thanks to reviewing the player play the game.

LIVE: LIVE WILL SCHOOL YOU

The Point

No matter what you thought you knew about how the game is going to be played, reviewed, or judged, you will be surprised, which means you have to be prepared to be schooled.

Further Definition

Have you ever been schooled before? I have and I'm not too proud to admit it. Sometimes the best thing we can do is admit that our conceptions are incorrect and grow from it. I bring this up because when a game goes live the world will come running at you full force. You thought just making the game was a herculean task, well, when it's live be prepared for the world to jump all over your life for good or ill.

Players will play your game in ways you never thought of doing it, break it in ways you never thought possible, complain/celebrate it to anyone who will listen, make online videos about it, review it, and hold discussions over any minute facet in online forums.

Reviewers will play only a few levels yet judge the whole game, focus more on clickbait attach rates for the story than on journalistic integrity, dole out a passing grade with no reasoning, take out their job dissatisfaction on your game, and reinvent the review wheel to literally explain one premise (play it or don't) in dizzying levels of complexity.

Technical issues will plague your every waking moment, with platforms going online or offline, randomly affecting player sentiment, along with servers dropping off when you least expect it and occurring at the worst of times. The number of people on a server bogs it down for everyone, forcing your game to be played at a crawl, and patches will cause more harm than good even though your team has tested them.

All of this and more may befall you, which means you need to let go of your control of things with the game and return to an old state I levied on you way back at the beginning of this journey. Learn to surf the chaos. Those who do, compartmentalizing each issue to be identified, evaluated, and fixed, will survive this period to live to develop again. I myself have seen a great many developers who were rock stars while developing the game crack under the world pressure when the game is live. Learn that it's not all on your shoulders, and that the best you can do is ride those waves.

Steps to Success

- Mentally prepare yourself for failure. Accept that it will happen and learn from it. Go ask out someone knowing you will be rejected and learn the rejection doesn't matter.
- Remember that reviewers are people too with human flaws, which means do not start a flame war with them. Be better.
- Learn to stick to your live operations staff, as they will have the pulse of the game.

LIVE: FIX THE BOAT BEFORE MAKING A NEW ONE

The Point

Fixing existing features in the game is more important than adding in new features.

Further Definition

This sounds simple, huh? Well, of course I would want to finish features and have all of the identified bugs fixed before I move on to another feature. If I had a broken feature and I added another feature on top of that, it has a great possibility of adding unneeded bugs into the product that could seriously hinder the enjoyment of the game for players. As a designer I would never think of doing such things … well, wake up and realize that this happens way more than anyone likes to admit.

Most of the time, producers/marketing drive the patches/DLC and want new features to hook people into the product along with looping in new players (note that other groups can lead this charge, but it's usually producers/marketing). Most of the time they will razzle-dazzle everyone with sales forecasts and the mighty needs of the players (most of whom they have never communicated with) for these features. As far as they are concerned, why would they fix something the player has already found tolerable as they have purchased the game? I have heard about every excuse in the book from engineers don't want to fix bugs to it will make the team unhappy forcing everyone to focus on new features. Basically they will try whatever excuse to get new features before fixing the product. It's not that they do not care, it's just that the lure of shiny new things is stronger than going back to clean up one's room. Cleaning up your room is about the last thing you want to do, especially if you have spent however long looking at your room in detail.

This means you need to be the shining vanguard of improving the game (fixing the boat) before you make new features (getting a new boat). Even when everyone wants to focus on the new, you need to be the one person who convinces everyone that the game will benefit from fixes first, which means you need to pitch your approach to anyone who will listen. Never say a flat no to everyone, just say, "Yes, but after …" which should keep them happy. In the end you as a designer might not have the final say, but it's your job to fight for the quality of the product, with QA at your shoulders like your hired goons to back you up. On many occasions, if your passionate pleas are not completely agreed to, you will still get some bugs fixed along with a few new features, which is a win—but The Point of the game is to get all identified issues fixed before new features. The quest is real, and I charge you with it.

Steps to Success

- Write up an elevator pitch for why bugs need to be fixed first.
- Pitch it to everyone that you can think of before you try it on the powers that be. Learn and refine your points.
- Pitch your points to the powers that be. Accept you might not win everything, but start with that to show you're open to negotiating down to a 50/50 split. Still a win.

LIVE: FROM TROLLS TO HEROES

The Point

No matter how you feel about people on the Internet, you need to respect the fact that we live in an age where a few passionate trolls can completely destroy a game before anyone can say, "Who was that masked man?"—which means you need to help convert them to being heroes.

Further Definition

Reviewers are one thing, but when you have a game out in the wide world you will encounter the unique form of humanity (I use humanity in the loosest of terms here) known as the Internet troll. This entitled subspecies will take it as their divine right to call out a game or designer about anything and everything in the game they didn't like or expect. Expectations are the hardest to deal with as they are normally where people who worked on a game get hurt the most. Marketing may have not been explicitly clear about what was being delivered or overhyped it to the point where if your game doesn't aid people to walk on water they call you out on the Internet as a piece of garbage.

What I've found is the best marketing approach to keep trolls at bay is clear representation of the product with no gilding of the lily. Let the product speak for itself. If you have a good game, that is your marketing. If you need marketing to push an angle, it's to cover up a poor product. No matter what marketing says, though, you can turn a troll into a hero—and deep down everyone wants to be a hero. To make this happen, you want to naturally create groundswell around a game, which will turn people from trolls who constantly detract into the heroes who fight for your game against any trolls. The more heroes you have, the more positive uptick you will get in the press and online. If a large group is writing, discussing, or raving about how great your game is, the player masses will undoubtedly follow. This conversion (or exorcism) can take many forms, but it largely has to do with respecting your game-playing populace by inviting them to see behind the curtain, answering their questions in a clear, entertaining manner, and celebrating them for enjoying your product. You can come up with many ways to support the product, as a designer might not always be just about the internal of the game but also have to support the external of the game. I myself was taught in the old-school manner where if you don't have something nice to say, don't say it—and on the Internet that goes doubly so, as it's there for all time.

Steps to Success

- Identify where your game is likely to be discussed by players from around the world and sign up on those sites as a member.
- Work out what you can do as a designer to respect the players enjoying your product in whatever form you can think of. Bounce it off the powers that be to see what sticks.
- Do one of the items you thought up to respect your players. They deserve it.

LIVE: A/B/C/D … Q TESTING

The Point

When your product is live, it's a smart idea to have some A/B testing options built in to improve the product.

Further Definition

A/B testing is the act of providing different players with different situations to test out which they like better. It's all about the hypothesis, the test, and the resulting numbers. This can be done to improve elements in, around, and outside of the game itself.

First, you need to work out the testing technology with the engineering group and what you want to test against. This can be between groups of players, locales in the world, or a percentage of the player base itself. Try to come up with the best grouping you're looking for first before diving in.

Next, you need to come up with the tests you want to run. This can be anything and everything inside or outside the game. At the heart of the test itself, you should be looking at verifying a hypothesis that you have to improve a facet of the game. From here, you need to work out the different variables in the test, the length of the intended test, along with the goal you're looking to achieve. This will give you the outline for the test itself that will allow you to share with other departments. Plus, you can be running multiple tests at the same time around different areas of the game. Just remember to be targeted in the tests instead of checking on everything.

Once you have the test, run it for the intended length and collect the results. When you get the numbers, be brave, because they won't always prove your hypothesis. This is where I tell you that every test—even if it disproves your hypothesis—is a lesson to be learned from as the player base will show you what they are really looking for. Once you get the data, look at it dispassionately to come to the best course of action to go forward with.

With the data collected, come up with the change that the data pointed toward to present to the other groups in development. Once everyone is on board, then you can work with them to develop the change into the game itself. In this way you have brought the player into the design process to help you improve the game. This tried and true method of testing can improve the game across every area if you set up the tests to do so. Just remember that data is dispassionate and without ego. It's there to help you learn. Love the data and always present it to everyone as a chance to learn, as that is truly what it is. Learn to love the data, as it can be most helpful to you in the long run.

Steps to Success

- Come up with an A/B test you want to run in some aspect of your life, with a hypothesis, length, and intended goal. Ask your friends to be the ones helping you with the test.
- Collect the results, share them with your friends who helped.
- Come up with improvements based on the data you have learned.

LIVE: DLC FOR YOU AND ME

The Point

DLC (downloadable content) is like its own mini-game and needs to be treated like its own product with a full (albeit reduced complexity) development cycle. The moment you start treating it as such, the better your game will be with some spanking new DLC.

Further Definition

DLC bundles a collection of bug fixes and new features/missions/levels that will be applied to the base game to add value as well as some extra revenue. Building out a DLC plan mashes together the development system from pre-production to release, yet it happens in one to six months. This means you have to be on your game as everything will be moving faster, and your calls will need to be rock solid, as you will undoubtedly have little to no time to go back to fix them.

The way I have seen DLC sell is based on a few tips I was shown early on. First, you need a clear, concise design that is even more refined than the elevator pitch for everyone to understand and that has very few moving parts. An example is like producing one major and three minor new features for a DLC instead of dozens of features. Most players just want extra love, which means it's on you to keep them excited as they want the extended edition rather than the director's cut.

Second, have everyone bought in on the vision for the DLC. There is nothing worse than people having different visions of the end product. I suggest when it's all solidified bring everyone into one meeting to learn the focus as well as to ask questions. This way everyone is on the same page to begin the development sprint to the finish line.

Third, resist putting more into the DLC, as much as you desperately want to. When the floodgates of fixes and new features open, people tend to have a nasty habit of throwing in as much of the kitchen sink as they can for a DLC. The best thing you can do is have everyone stick to the plan, and if there is any extra time, use that to polish what you have.

My personal favorite DLC of all time just took an amazing game and added zombies to it with a new story, which was genius that laid a new aspect on a game that already was best of breed. Sometimes it's the simplest things that will make a DLC the reason for players who might have skipped your title to purchase it—and the reason for players who might have put the game down to play it again.

Steps to Success

- Chart the three best DLCs and learn why they were successful, then apply that.
- Come up with a clear vision of a DLC that can be explained in one sentence.
- Make a presentation that explains the DLC goals with text and visuals.

LIVE: WORKFLOW WAVES

The Point

Live period workflow is more like waves in an ocean instead of peaks and valleys in a development system. It's a very different world to keep yourself motivated in, as there isn't always a sense of urgency.

Further Definition

While I've spoken before in previous points about workflow in development periods that feels like you're sprinting to the finish line, in live you need to learn to have a constant state of issues, work, and (on many occasions) time to finish what you need. I am always shocked that in the live period my work is much more like a smooth wave undulating from medium to high levels, which is a refreshing change from nothing to maximum amounts of work.

I've known many designers who don't understand how to behave with their world set to medium when they only know maximum. Some actually screw up more during this period as they don't attack issues with the same fervor or their fix success rate drops. It sounds funny, but it's really true that when a person is used to running on all cylinders they actually find themselves wandering aimlessly in circles due to not having any urgency to finish a task. The best I can say to you is that you need to learn to juggle this life just like you did in the development cycle.

Even though there might not be the urgency you're used to, it's good to keep yourself on an even keel in this period. Best way to do this is to set yourself daily goals and stick to them. I've seen myself and many designers flourish in this period because we have work to keep us busy along with the ability to have an outside life. It's a glorious time—you just need to remember that work needs to get done to support a release.

Oh, and learn a very important skill: GO HOME, HAVE A LIFE, BE HAPPY. This is what the normal people have every five days a week with this mythical time period they call weekends. Like them, you now have the chance to rekindle your life, connect with friends and family, apologize to your significant other if they are still around (I've seen too many relationships explode due to games development hours and stress). You will be able to enjoy hobbies again or the simple act of reading a book for no reason other than it looks like a bit of fun. All of these things you need to get back into, and this is a great time for you to recharge. That doesn't mean falling down (that's a worst-case scenario), but actually going back to normal is a celebrated thing you need to enjoy.

Steps to Success

- Set yourself a daily plan of action and stick to it. GET 'ER DONE!
- Make a point of reconnecting with at least one outside-of-work friend.
- LEAVE THE OFFICE. Walk outside and take the weight off your shoulders that has to do with work. It feels great to leave work at the door.

CHAPTER 10

Miscellaneous

CONTENTS

Level 0: Miscellaneous	208
Miscellaneous or Everything Else	210
Miscellaneous: The Written Word	211
Miscellaneous: The Powerless Um	212
Miscellaneous: Presentation Preparation	214
Miscellaneous: Art of the Presentation	215
Miscellaneous: Storytelling	216
Miscellaneous: Silent but Deadly	217
Miscellaneous: Interface Design	219
Miscellaneous: Systems Designers	220
Miscellaneous: Content Designers	221
Miscellaneous: Level Designers	223
Miscellaneous: Audio Designers	224
Miscellaneous: See-Mores	225
Miscellaneous: 30-Day Design Challenge	227

LEVEL 0: MISCELLANEOUS

You might think it's your skill tree and gear in a game that make you a great, powerful character, yet it's not all about what you can see that makes you great. It's actually all about what you do using your intelligence, wisdom, and experience that makes you a wonder in a game. While each game has its own set of trials, there are a few miscellaneous skills you should remember to take note of for all games.

One of the best skills to remember is the metaphorical sharpening of your blade. Many believe that just gaining a sword gives them the ability to destroy, but if you have ever picked up a sword before you will realize that the feeling of power disappears when you try to hack the air with the skill of a child who has watched a pirate movie. No grace, no skill, and just a feeling that you can crush something if you wanted. What you need to understand is that it takes countless hours of practice, education, and mentoring to learn to wield a sword successfully. You need to realize that gaining the sword is only the first step instead of the last step. Plus, when you get a sword, I highly recommend you check how sharp it is, as this is a very important factor that most overlook when getting one. You need to sharpen a sword to cut, and you need to remember that keeping it sharp is important. The sword is your mind if you haven't guessed already.

Another skill to understand is that you can transcend classes to survive from game to game. You might think that knowing how to be a medic or a sniper will keep you alive, but I'm here to tell you that this will only keep you adept in a specific game's genre, which won't last forever. To explain further, envision you're the best race car driver in the world. You can handle any road. Yet when a bloodthirsty horde of zombies appears over the horizon and you only have a shotgun, it's time to rethink all the time you spent driving in circles. Both are specific classes that will achieve success on their own, but you need to look at them as skills instead of classes. You can have many skills in your life, and they are yours to fashion together through practice to create your experience. What I'm here to explain is that knowing just one is a false statement and whenever given the chance you should be expanding what you know to be the ultimate badass. Learn to combine skills so that one day you're a sniping medic race car driver who speeds through levels in your gleaming car firing a shotgun into any hapless zombie that happens to get in your way.

The last great skill I can mention is picking the right allies. These people, either in work or outside of work, as friends or family, are the ones who keep you sane when the game tries to destroy you. Without them you can't survive, which means you need to pick them well, like you would a party to go adventuring with. This means removing the crappy outside-of-work people from your life—you have better things to do than waste your time on them—and inside of work figure out who to surround yourself with to keep you happy every day. These simple guidelines will help you keep your social circles clean and joyful, just what you need in support from your allies against what any game can

throw at you. If you have these points mastered, you have completed level zero.

MISCELLANEOUS OR EVERYTHING ELSE

The Point

Being a designer and surviving a game are not all about the game. No, I'm not trying to be all "walking against the wind," I'm just stating that there are outside areas to focus on as well to help aid you in your survival.

Further Definition

Now, this section is specifically to fill in all of the outside points that a designer should learn if and when given the chance. These points are for you to know how to do no matter what period of the development cycle the product is in. You should be adding these tools to your already awesome collection of skills to make you a better all-around designer instead of just a one-hit wonder. The well-rounded designer can jump to any position, job or company with agile ease which makes them the more valuable asset to any game.

It scares the crap out of me that designers are now being compartmentalized into subgroups that don't even deal with each other properly throughout the project and at the end only have experienced the small area they were told to focus on. While I understand it's helpful for junior designers to do this, I'm now seeing it turn into an industry norm where level designers are now senior and lead level designers, never having any effect on other parts of the project. My personal version of being a designer is simply this: "You are the jack of all trades, master of none, but better than everyone else at a wide array of skills for the benefit of the game." (Don't forget you are in service to it, as the game keeps you in a vocation.) The sad part about this is that games keep getting bigger, taking longer to build, and just plain requiring more humans to get accomplished, forcing the fracture of the designer family into many shards that have truly forgotten what it's like to be the whole.

This is why old designers tend to focus on smaller games, because that way they get to offer everything of themselves to the job they love. I myself found that I started to gravitate away from the massive AAA titles that would suck up years of my life, as they had too many egos, too many working parts that became way too complicated for any one person to handle. Instead I learned that outside the world I thought I needed was where I would truly find my happiness—and you can too.

Steps to Success

- If you are a designer with a subsequent tag beside your title (level, systems, FE, etc.), pick up another discipline in your spare time and master it (1,000 hours of doing).
- Work at it. Work harder at it. Work until you can't think straight, and you will succeed. (Again, 1,000 hours will do that for you.)
- No matter how much you know about something, there is someone else who knows more. So stow your ego and continue to learn without barriers. Bow, don't scream.

MISCELLANEOUS: THE WRITTEN WORD

The Point

Understanding that you are a writer is the first step. Understanding you're not a great writer is the next. Finally, practicing writing to make yourself better is the lesson we all need to learn.

Further Definition

Your writing is one of the best tools you need to understand, regurgitate, and have sing to anyone that comes close to it. If you don't have this skill down, go take a class online or at any school. Understanding the written language and how to manipulate it is an art form that people strive for worldwide and has been a magnificent pursuit since we as a species first thought to do it.

As a designer you should want this ability as much as a professional writer. For millennia, people have been working at the written word to make sense of their experiences for others. As a designer who is crafting new worlds for people to experience, you have to be able to do that with multiple limbs tied behind your back along with being blindfolded (I haven't decided if you should be dancing too, but you get the point). If a player could only play your written words, what would the review score for your game be? Think about it like that and you will start to understand how important this is. Plus, on many occasions your written words will need to woo people you have never met to follow or support your game. The better your skills are at this, the better you will aid your games.

Personally, I try to spend part of each week writing just for myself to upgrade my skill outside of any work. Then when a piece is completed I pass it along to a friend to review. I have routinely sought out a wonderful person with writing skill far above of my own to read my works, as I find that I'm always trying to improve my work to maybe one day make it to the level of their own uncommon creations. I'll always keep trying and you should as well. Just do me this one favor: unless you're writing a full-fledged novel, learn to let an idea go and move on to something else. There is nothing as sad as a writer gripping onto a story he or she can't finish. Write anything, but always remember that the goal is to finish it.

Steps to Success

- Write for yourself at least once a week on any topic for a minimum of one hour in whatever format you think best works for you.
- If you know your writing isn't up to par, take a class in creative writing. Learning is fun and you can always learn more.
- Learn to love the written word. A designer at any level needs to know how to manipulate ideas, so learn from great writers you look up to. (In other words, read more.)

MISCELLANEOUS: THE POWERLESS UM

The Point

You might think this funny, but "um" leads to many humans' downfall through mistrust, and many of us use it daily without actually realizing it.

Further Definition

"Um" is the word that most English-speaking people use when they haven't taken the time to know the statement they wish to deliver, they want to add more information without taking a second to think about it, or think they need to add more information to justify their statements. To the trained ear, this leads to people mistrusting your statements and intentions, which leads to people no longer trusting you know what you're talking about. It's a slippery slope and I have seen many developers lose the faith of people around them by just using this little word, even though they are very capable of greatness. They just don't communicate it properly.

"Um" can always be avoided, you just have to train yourself to not use it. This can be done in a few ways and should be something that you focus on. One method is by having your statements thought out in advance. This isn't always possible, but there are predictive interactions that you can prepare for. A daily morning meeting, for example, is a predictive situation. I always use the KISS system—keep it simple, stupid. I plan what I'm going to say in short, quick statements that leave it open for further questions if needed. If questions are asked, I reply in short, specific statements again to save everyone time. This formulation of thoughts and statements will help you avoid adding unneeded information. Another way to subjugate the "um" is to have confidence that your statements don't need further justification. You have to impress no one except yourself. This sounds easy but can be difficult for many who don't feel confident in their daily lives. We are not robots that react the same every day, but in situations when we are being asked for information, updates, or our opinions it's better to speak with simple, straightforward language to show others that we can be trusted without "um" in between.

I've actually seen this be the difference between leaders and followers in many games I've worked on. The leaders speak with confidence, and the followers stammer over their words, adding "um" to attempt to justify their language. This doesn't mean that the confident statements given by leaders are always right, but the delivery helps everyone understand that they have it thought out. The ones who haven't focused on this doom themselves to being passed over for opportunities, all based around a little word like "um."

Steps to Success

- The next time you're in a meeting or with friends, watch how many times "um" is used in the conversation.
- Record yourself in a meeting or with friends (with their permission, of course) and review it to hear how many times you use "um."
- The next time someone asks you how your day is going, have three specific short statements to reply with instead of thinking about it.

MISCELLANEOUS: PRESENTATION PREPARATION

The Point

Presentations are one of the greatest tools a designer has to show off to a population what they are thinking. It's a light version of the standard pitch documentation in a format that everyone understands.

Further Definition

Presentations are really quite difficult but with a little guidance you can start to master this art. To do this you need to understand the fundamentals of preparation, simplicity, bells and whistles, and performance.

First is preparation, where you need to find a presentation program and learn its many facets as perfectly as possible. This program should want to take you out on a date, you know it so well, and have your children when you're not even looking. You will also need content, which means you need some written word and a boatload of stunning visuals.

Second has to do with simplicity, and I can tell you already that you've used too many slides and way too much text. (How do I know? That's the way everyone starts.) You need to plan out your message like a story that hooks the reader on page one, builds up the story with some mystery, culminates in a dizzying climax, and then gently tucks you in at the end, safe that all you know is correct. This should be done in the fewest amount of slides (think 3, 5, 7, 11 slides max), using the fewest written words or statements that corroborate what you will be speaking.

Thirdly, you need to add all the bells and whistles to the presentation, from anything involving music to video and even role-play—being a character can make you into a hero even if you don't feel like one. And let it not be understated that some smart clothing will do in a pinch, as every knight needs their armor. Next, you need to create a handout for the people to look through during the presentation, discuss when referring to specific points, and take away with them when the performance is done (yes, it is a performance). Personally, I put some effort into the handout as it's something they will review—the higher quality, the better.

Lastly is the performance itself. You need to organize the proper space for the presentation and prepare your vocal performance. This means practice with your body language, verbal cues, and timing. These are not skills many are taught, so spend some time to learn them now. If you incorporate all of these things together and focus on having answers for any questions that might come, you will give a great presentation.

Steps to Success

- Create a game idea and write it up along with some visuals.
- Transfer that information into a slide presentation that you practice on others.
- Create a handout for the presentation that would make marketing people weep at its beauty and majesty (and no, that isn't a printout of the presentation).

MISCELLANEOUS: ART OF THE PRESENTATION

The Point

The presentation itself is an art. If you ever question that, go look online at some great orators who make it look easy. They themselves practiced it more times than they would care to admit.

Further Definition

What I can bestow on you is to practice and focus on being center stage, be calm as a cucumber until you don't need to be, and know your audience. I know this sounds like simple advice, but it's actually really difficult for people to get these skills down. It doesn't mean you can't, it just means (like many things) it takes a lot of practice.

To be center stage is to know you're up there as the focal point, the main attraction, and that means you need to be the entertainment everyone came to see. You're not presenting dry quarterly sales figures. You need to use your voice to enrapture the people attending your performance (yes, you are a performer, so act like one). Similar to the elevator pitch, you need to use the minimum amount of words to hook your audience, leaving them the space to fill in the gaps, as no one likes being told what to think.

Next, you need to learn to find your calm when everyone is looking at you to be the ringmaster of this three-ring circus they have been invited to. It's a difficult thing, and the only way I can explain to get over this difficulty is to stand up in front of a group and use your oratory skills any chance you get. Professional actors have this ability because they have done nothing but practice it. They failed, got back up, and kept doing it until they are the paragons that the populace looks up to, forcing awards into their hands every chance we get. All of this said, there is a place for calm and there is a place for emotional revelry. This means your passion has to be shown to the audience without you being thought of a fanatic for the core concept. Some of the best presenters I've seen picked the moments when they wanted everyone to feel their words' impact through their passion.

Lastly, try your hardest to know your audience beforehand and tailor your presentation to the ears of the people present. It does you no good to explain details to closed minds. You need to know what makes your audience tick and customize your message to them—remember, you're looking for the maximum effect in the shortest possible time. Wow them and leave them wanting more. It never hurts to take an encore bow if they are begging for it, but that is hubris talking.

Steps to Success

- Practice using your voice by enunciating every word, speaking with authority. Enjoy being the main attraction.
- When you have created a presentation, do many, many, many dry runs before you attack your target audience. Practice makes perfect and will ease you into it.
- Wow with every slide, and leave some room to let your audience fill in the gaps. Remember, you're selling this, so remind them they can't live without it.

MISCELLANEOUS: STORYTELLING

The Point

One of my favorite storytelling quotes comes from a television program I saw when I was little and had an outstanding impact on me: "When people told themselves their past with stories, explained their present with stories, foretold the future with stories, the best place by the fire was kept for … the Storyteller." You want to be that storyteller.

Further Definition

The art of storytelling is just that—an art. The sooner you realize that any game you're making has a narrative to it, the better your games will be and the better your skill in this area. Storytelling by definition is the conveying of events in words, images, and sounds, but that's just basic idea of what it truly is. Stories have been shared since the beginning of time by every culture as a means of entertainment, education, and cultural preservation.

Crucial elements of stories and storytelling include plot, characters, and narrative point of view, all of which you will need to learn to master.

Many games suffer from a total lack of storytelling, and many have just tried to simplify the story to its barest bones level. I have been told that games don't need stories and the player only wants to play without being told a narrative. That is garbage, as every game has its own story that hooks the player even if you haven't learned what it is yet. People by nature want to be told a story or create one themselves. Don't let anyone tell you that video games aren't a medium for art as they are a brilliant medium for storytelling.

As a designer, you must learn to tell stories better than anyone else and create a mythos behind your products to help them succeed. It's not just enough to have a great story, that story needs to be translated into a games format and hold up every step of the way. This is a hard task, as proven by a multitude of craptastic games where the player spends more time buttoning through the story instead of paying attention, just to get to the next gameplay sequence. You need to learn to make players care and that means being a better storyteller. If you can do that, you will have a rabid fan base that will never leave you.

Many years ago, I was taught by a wonderful mentor that the best designer in the room is the one who can tell the best story. It doesn't matter if it's true or false—it just has to be believed so completely by everyone that they look to the storyteller as the only source of truth. That truth will indoctrinate them to whatever cause you express.

Steps to Success

- Practice telling your friends great stories. Anyone's stories.
- Pick the top five games you have found that are great at storytelling and figure out what made them great stories.
- Take a recent game you know that failed the storytelling mark and rewrite it to make the narrative sing.

MISCELLANEOUS: SILENT BUT DEADLY

The Point

Your words are powerful, but you need to learn to use them sparingly. No one will listen to you if you're spouting off all the time.

Further Definition

Many designers I have known suffer from verbal diarrhea where they feel the need to talk all the time to fill in all of the gaps. Added to this, in the beginning of their career many junior designers think that they need to speak up as much as possible in a vain attempt to show everyone that they are skilled. The real joke is that it's totally the opposite—they know very little and they prove that to the senior designers when they can't stop talking.

What you need to expand on is what I call the sacred art of being silent and deadly. This art starts with knowing that you're okay. Yes, it's that easy, but I can bet you don't feel okay with yourself. You first need to understand that you don't have to impress anyone, and the only person you need to fight daily is yourself. Some days you'll win and some days you won't. Learn that self-doubt is your only enemy and you will start to be okay.

Next, you just need to learn to speak less. You don't always need to have the answers. You don't need to let others know your feelings on every subject or make them understand that your point of view is correct. You can just learn to let arguments that do not matter truly slide off your back and carry on with a life that focuses on issues that really matter to you. All those little points you feel the need to speak about do not matter.

Along with speaking less, you have to listen better and be an active listener. An active listener requires that the listener fully concentrate, understand, respond, and then remember what is being said. This is very important, as this is how the speaker knows that you are connected with what they are saying instead of just waiting for your time to speak. One way to help actively listen, I have found, is to take notes. Notes can be revisited when the speaker is done, and they show you have been paying attention, coupled with showing respect for the speaker by waiting and allowing them to get their point across.

The last part of this art is making sure you pick the right words in the right combination to have the maximum effect. Avoid wishy-washy statements and focus on absolutes that lead people. I've found that the best way for me to formulate this is to take a breath and collect my words into the sentence I want to deliver, saying it once in my head for effect before I say it out loud.

Steps to Success

- The next conversation you have, say less and watch yourself doing it.
- Next meeting, practice being an active listener taking notes.
- Next time you want to speak, plan your sentence before you speak it.

MISCELLANEOUS: INTERFACE DESIGN

The Point

The presentation of menus and how a player interacts with them is a massively important part of games and deserves your respect as much as any back-end gameplay feature.

Further Definition

Interface design is most often the newbie job for a designer and something that suffers more times than I can recall in all games. That said, many games are now hiring interface designers to make their games better, but that comes after many years of menu systems that caused players to throw controllers at their screens instead of playing their games. You would think that the few front-end screens you need to pass through and the little bit of in-game menus would be an easy gig, but you would be wrong. Creating a well-thought-out menu system is a feat all to itself and needs more focus than people give it credit for. If you disagree, go to any of your favorite websites and realize that they have perfected a superior menu system to get you to the content you most desire.

You need to have a solid base in two-dimensional design, layout, functionality, and usability, which takes schooling as far as I'm concerned. It can be learned from books and practical experience, yet I've found the best interface designers learned it from schooling. This is because we as a species have many generations of experience in this, and it's best to learn from historical mistakes than doom yourself to do them again in a new medium. It is also something that in our three-dimensional world of games has become a forgotten art form, like writing in cursive (do you even know what cursive is?). Not only does a designer need to understand how every screen fits together, looks, and functions appropriately (with the great help of the coding and art staff), you need to see the big picture of how it relates directly with gameplay.

As much as games are removing in-game menus and elements these days, people still require that visual cue to know what's going, which makes interface designers' skill set immensely important. Unfortunately, the best an interface designer can hope for is that when you have done your job right, no one notices it because they have already dismissed it from their minds to enjoy the gameplay experience (sad, I know, but true). That doesn't mean you should give it any less respect. The secret goal of any game designer is to have the player so happy with the gameplay experience they don't even notice your hand in it.

Steps to Success

- Take your favorite website and chart out the flow of the design with each screen and how they are connected to each other.
- Do a simple one-screen layout for the main menu screen for one of your game ideas, utilizing layout, functionality, and usability.
- Take your favorite in-game interface and figure out why all of the elements on screen really work.

MISCELLANEOUS: SYSTEMS DESIGNERS

The Point

Systems designers are the blood that keeps the body moving. They are the masters of the little things that govern everything inside a game.

Further Definition

Inside the systems is the magic no one ever sees, no one ever thinks about, but without the systems we would all fall apart. The numbers, and the finely tuned manipulation of those numbers, are what makes magic work inside of a game. Whether it's a gun that shoots bullets or a car that can take any turn at speed, it's all done by a systems designer.

Unlike many designers, the systems designer is closest to an engineer as they are almost completely obsessed with logic, numbers, and systems within systems. It's typically a job most people don't want, as it's more science than art, but the right people in the right headspace can make a game shine. It's a valuable art to understand all of the variables and keep them in one's head to balance a product.

To understand what it takes to be a systems designer, you first have to come to terms with mathematics and the application of math in a virtual world, which until one sets up the systems and boundaries is no good to anyone—the player will reject the world unless it conforms to a logic they themselves hold to. As an example, think of a sword. It's metal, a certain length, sharp, a weapon and held to be used. Unlike a content designer, the systems designer takes these variables and affixes values to them. This allows permutations to occur where the sword can be of multiple lengths, metals, sharpness, etc. From there, they can build out charts to figure out what sword should be offered to the player at each point of the game, in concert with the content designers. No one expects the best sword in the first level—they would grow bored cutting swaths through enemies with little difficulty. Instead, they expect to get a dull short sword that they will have to work with in the hope of gaining a better one later on. The systems designer chooses when you get the better sword—and why it's better—through systems they have created using numbers to balance the equation of "sword." Now think about this with every possible weapon a game has along with how these weapons interact with each other. You're starting to understand the complexity part with just one weapon.

Depending on the game, these systems can be everything inside of the world that interacts with the player's experience, and it's a difficult thing to keep working harmoniously together. One variable changed can be catastrophic if done incorrectly. It's a game of balance.

Steps to Success

- Take any item and break it up into all of its possible variables.
- Take your wardrobe, enter it into a systems program, and plan your next outfit.
- Find a book on systems—any systems in life—and learn from it. It takes a unique mind to think with this style of logic.

MISCELLANEOUS: CONTENT DESIGNERS

The Point

Content designers are the ones in charge of adding the special sauce to a game that would otherwise be just meat and vegetables.

Further Definition

Not all companies have content designers, and on many occasions I have seen level designers expected to fill in this job—but that doesn't mean they are any good at it. Content is itself a part of the game that needs to be respected. Content makes up two specific areas: items for the player to utilize and items in the levels themselves. Both are important, as they are the tool box given to players and the objects added to the world the player will inhabit.

Items for the players can be anything that the player can use in situations in the game, from jump functionality to a spaceship and everything in between. If the player can use it, it's content, and you would be amazed that designers can spend all of their days on something as simple as a sword. At the same time, you need to understand that a great functioning sword can make or break a game, as no one wants to swing a crappy sword repeatedly.

The items in the world are another area that most people don't think about but need to have to fill in the game environment. A great way to visualize this is to think about moving into a new place. At first, it's a blank canvas, devoid of habitation, but when you unpack everything and fill in the space, it becomes a home to be treasured. Without the things, it's only four walls and misses the point. Content in the game world adds the little special touches that connect the player with the world they are in. That means it's the content designer's focus to make the world habitable, real, and sustainable with the objects at their disposal. That said, placing a boatload of crates in a level is not good content design, it's cheating. Don't be THAT content designer.

Player content is typically one of the first things thought of when designing a game, with environmental content being the last added, largely due to the art side needing to build out the levels before the designer can get to the tuning. Each can be done with a purpose or it can be done, as I like to term it, higgledy-piggledy. I think you know which side I fall on. Having a thought pattern and decision matrix thought out for the content is a way to guarantee a solid game experience. This is an area where the devil lives in the details and the details are king. The smallest variable can mean the difference between a well-received game, a game people complain about for years to come, or worst of all a game everyone has forgotten. If only they had added a little special sauce.

Steps to Success

- Take any object and work out all the ways to use it. What are the optimum ways to use it?
- Take any room of your home and remaster it for the space.
- Make dinner for yourself. Document what objects and environment you used to complete it. Now, what could you do to perfect it all?

MISCELLANEOUS: LEVEL DESIGNERS

The Point

Level design is the minutiae of the gameplay experience from beat to beat and makes up the gameplay experience every player enjoys.

Further Definition

Level design is a blanket term for design that deals directly with the environments of a game for the creation of levels, stages, and/or missions. I have known people who call themselves level designers and create the level from scratch using paper and modeling tools. On the other side, I know level designers who use level editing tools to place in every single mission object and completion criteria triggers. Both are the same but just start at different periods of the design from the conceptual stage to the brute implementation. Knowing how to build your own levels and script a situation into them is a very important skill for all games.

As long as you remember that level design is only a part of the entire design, you will be all right. It's something that most people can pick up pretty fast, as a multitude of the games on the market will give a crash course on what to do properly. I want to be clear—it's easy to pick up but a lifetime of practice to get right. I know only one rock-star level designer, and I bow to his amazing experience. He sees every environment as possibilities, like a sculptor seeing a block of marble and knowing that a masterpiece exists beneath the pieces he chips away. If I were to take away anything from this juggernaut of level design I would say a strong understanding of architecture and city planning is what level designers need to learn from. There is a massive amount of knowledge around those pursuits already in books and other media. The only difference between that rock star and traditional architects is that he sees the world as what could be rather than what it is supposed to be. That makes him a magician among mortals.

I really wanted to bring this point up to remind you to put some cycles around this area because the knowledge of it can make or break gameplay, which means even if you're not in charge of it you had better understand it to help out your game. Furthermore, you need to understand the level design theory of your game to implement it properly. It's no good to have a level design for a space marines game inside a present-day military shooter. A thought behind the thinker is the most important of traits to possess. The last bit I can say on this is learn pacing for each style of game, treating each level like a book with an opening, climax, and ending. If you have this down, your levels will shine.

Steps to Success

- Do research on different styles of level design and pacing for each of them from games you admire. Plot them out.
- Find the greatest level design tool and practice until your fingers bleed.
- Create your own level with the tool, then play it, and get someone else to play it in front of you, telling you what they think.

MISCELLANEOUS: AUDIO DESIGNERS

The Point

Audio designers are the masters of sound and the key masters to one of our most beloved senses.

Further Definition

Audio designers come up with the entire soundscape for the game, from the smallest button sounds to the greatest head-banging musical track that plays at just the right time to make every player go "HELL, YEAH!" Unfortunately, the sad reality is audio is usually left out of the mix (yes, pun intended) by game designers as they typically come from a different gamecentric background. True sound designers are audiophiles and speak the language of sound rather than traditional design. I have known more programmers who go into the sound field than traditional designers, but that's not to say it can't be done. The best audio designer I've known was someone who had been a musician since childhood and who cared more about a beautiful musical track than a video game.

Like most design areas, the art of sound can be taught, but it first needs to be a calling, as it routinely is not part of the classic education of game design. You must have an ear for it and that can sometimes not be trained. You've heard the joke about the tone-deaf sound designer … no, well, of course you haven't because they don't exist. That said, these people are just as important as any artist and programmer as they labor to bring the entire audio sense to life. Not just life but to sing, as a beautiful soundscape in a game can make all the difference. If you have played any game where this is done right, you would agree with me that the sound makes you connect more with everything going on in the game.

To test this, have you ever tried watching your favorite scene of a movie without all of the audio bells and whistles behind it? It really destroys the total emotional experience and feels like you have just been given a rotten apple instead of the feast for the senses you have been used to. You should respect this and learn to incorporate it into your design at all parts during the game's development. It's a very true statement that a great audio designer can mean the difference between a well-reviewed title and a bargain-binner. Audio is something every review includes in the game's total score as it's something everyone can understand.

Steps to Success

- Listen to the sounds of your favorite games. Take note of them all.
- Start watching movies with impressive sound design and research the extras section on the audio of the film to learn more.
- There is a great variety of free audio mixers on the web to make your own sounds and music. Download one to try it out. Learn to play, and learn how to create with your ears uncovered.

MISCELLANEOUS: SEE-MORES

The Point

Respect the people you work with, as the golden rule applies to work as it does with life. Treat others with respect and you will receive it in return.

Further Definition

Before the end, I thought I should add a point about treating other developers with respect. In any creative pursuit, egos come out of the woodwork on day one and people's feelings can get hurt quickly, which means you need to be the bigger person in almost every situation. This is harder than you will expect, and it's an art I'm learning to this day. Any business, especially a creative business, brings out people without any creativity whom you would rather not deal with. They are trained in traditional business and end up being leaders as they speak the language of money (not art). Art doesn't make money until it makes massive money and then everyone joins up.

I call the ego people "See-Mores." It's my own blanket term for them that reminds me these people take extra effort. Most See-Mores I have dealt with are extraordinarily bad at their jobs, cost their companies millions, and spend more time playing a political game than making the game itself. These people are never alone and are flanked by their sidekicks (I like to call them "Robins") who do a lot of the See-More's dirty work, keeping them in power. The scary part about them is that these people tend to jump ship after they have burned every bridge and then sell themselves as winners to the next unfortunate company they join, with a higher wage to boot. These people are dangerous and should be treated like rabid dogs in a dark alley. Don't antagonize, protect yourself, and have something on them that won't let them execute you for their own personal gain.

For a great period of my development history, I used to loathe these people openly to my own downfall. I had to learn that these people are at their core just uncomfortable in their own skins, as they are driven by the two greatest of human drives: fear and laziness. As a designer, it's your job to figure out how to deal with these people, not just dismiss them, which involves you figuring out what YOU can do to make the relationship better. It's tough to be the better person, but it's on you to suffer them until the day they are revealed like the emperor who has no clothes. I used to have a picture hanging at my desk with the Latin inscription "Ego Autem Ignium Durare"—in English, "I will outlast you," Only one See-More ever asked about it, and on the day he was let go for gross incompetence I raised a glass with him (instead of because of him) as he at least tried to change his spots.

Steps to Success

- Identify who the See-Mores and the Robins are in your life.
- Seek these people out and connect with them, as much as that might be very hard.
- Develop and maintain a relationship with See-Mores where they can't live without you. Manipulate the manipulators to survive.

MISCELLANEOUS: 30-DAY DESIGN CHALLENGE

The Point

It only takes 30 days to change your stars. If you focus on it instead of wasting your time with trivialities, you can achieve great things, and the people who do will enrich the world with wonder that it deserves.

Further Definition

The 30-day design challenge is the last gift I have to offer you and where you get to put all of your knowledge to the test. If you haven't figured it out, this book is about understanding and doing. In 30 days, make a game. But wait, you have already started thinking, games are too big and involve too many people to make in just 30 days—well, that just isn't always true. What you can do is think big, act small. By that I mean go find yourself a simple 2-D platformer tool on the web and make your own creation in just 30 days. Don't get tied up that it has to be an AAA title, because some of the best things come in the littlest packages, and I can name dozens of games made small that end up massive. They all started with an ember of creativity.

Like I have taught you already, break it all down to build it up again. For the first week, learn the tools you will need to the best of your ability while thinking up a game concept. Then break up the game's development into the next three weeks from Blue Sky to final in a simple schedule, recognizing that it might only be a few days for each of the development periods. That's where the challenge comes into play. Then put that plan into action and turn out a game.

Creation is miraculous, and anyone can do it. At the very least, you will have created something you can use for your portfolio and something tangible to show yourself that you can do it when put to the test. In your lowest moments, you will need to remind yourself you have created something real, and this is a great example, which is why I suggest trying it. Creative people need positive reinforcement wherever possible.

Anyone can do it … it just takes the will to make sure it gets done. Completion is a powerful statement in and of itself. Design is not about sitting still, it's about practically getting the job done. I hope that you can take everything you have learned in this book to help you set yourself up to make awesome games the world has yet to even dream of. And dammit, I'm excited to see what you come up with. If a single person does any of the Steps to Success I have laid out or gleams further understanding from my experience, then I have succeeded and the world is better for it. Be the next light of the world as a designer and make me proud without even knowing your name. You are capable of greatness … you just don't know it yet.

Steps to Success

- Find a tool to make the game and think up a great idea.
- Put all of the game information into a schedule and act on it.
- Finally, make the game. The act of creation has no comparison. Be great.

Conclusion

Congratulations! You have made it through every page and its wisdom has come to an end. (I'll know if you got here and didn't read every page. You know who you are, cheater.) When I started this, I really didn't know what it would turn into by the end, and with the support of the people around me it has come to this conclusion. I personally have learned I have a lot more to relate than I first expected. The first draft I wrote had 25 total pages, which I suspected would make a good post on a design website to educate fellow designers. Over time, and falling into a wonderful group to work with, I realized I had more to express, which caused the page count to swell. Then with editing I brought it back down to a size that made the most sense, making the porridge just right.

There is always more to say on this subject, and I'm not arrogant enough to think I got every possible point. Like everyone on this spinning ball of dirt, I am fallible and have much learning to do myself, yet for the person that I am now this is what I have to offer you to support you being better. Learning to accept our limitations is very important, and knowing that to win we first need to fail a lot. This stumble and fall routine I have lived for my entire career has taught me to focus on picking myself up to help where I can, even if it means my own demise.

Please take what you have learned from this book, practice as much as you can whenever you can, and add to it from your own experience. Grow from what you are now after reading this, and I hope that now that you're done you use this as a reference guide to pull from to help with any point during your adventures in design. The art of improvement is something I hope you have gotten into your skull as the only way to be better—we rarely stumble into perfection without trying. No matter what media tells us, we need to work at it, and I have found the journey is worth more than the end goal.

If you are ever done with this tome, pass it along, as this is knowledge to share and not hoard (not to be resold … I will know and don't think I won't curse you). This was one of the main reasons I wrote this book—I was sick of game designers keeping these secrets to themselves to help guarantee they would survive. Knowledge needs to be shareable. We can all learn something from being transparent and passing on our great adventures to others for them to learn from. For good or ill, for success or failure, we are not fools, so why should we repeat our mistakes? Pass this book on for others to learn.

Lastly, because this is me and I like to put a pin in things, I would like to take this moment to thank you for reading this. It means a lot to me. Without knowing your face or name, I'm happy to help you out with a little piece of my experience to aid you in making better video games. Now it's time for you to take what you have learned, knock it out of the park on your game, and live to make more games. No one can stop you but you, which means put your demons aside through knowledge and WIN. Create greatness, practice hard, surround yourself with all the world has to offer, and make great games.

Index

2-D camera. *See* Two-dimensional (2-D) camera
2-D platformer tool, 227
3-D camera. *See* Three-dimensional (3-D) camera
30-day design challenge, 227–228
100% fix rate, 120–121, *See also* Bugs
125% fix rate, 119–120, *See also* Bugs

A

A/B testing, 201–202
Active listener, 218
Allies, 209–210, *See also* Social circles
Alpha, 114–141
- asking for help, 125–126
- bugs, *See* Bugs
- building/cultivating followers, 136–137
- concept, 116–117
- demos, 137–138
- early-access offering, 138–139
- helping others, 127–129
- milestones, racing towards, 126–127
- overtime madness, 129–130
- overview, 114–115
- pivoting, art of, 130–131
- quality assurance (QA), 132–133
- test/testing, 123–124
- trend followed for design change, 133–134
- updating design, 134–135
- *you* time/moment, 140–141

Alpha period, 103
Arcade game, 30
Architecting a fix, 180
Artificial intelligence (AI), 101–103
Ask for help, 125–126
Asking questions. *See* Question/ questioning oneself
Audience
- presentation and, 216
- target, 32–33
- writing design for, 44–45

Audio design, 57–58
Audio designers, 155, 224–225
Audiophiles, 224

B

Backstory, 46–47
Balance/balancing, 80–81
Beta, 144–161
- concept, 146–147
- "herding cats," 156–157
- knowing the game, 150–151
- monotony, dealing with, 152–153
- offering assistance and fix for bugs, 148–149
- overview, 144–145
- player setting/location, 154–155
- playing the game, 153–154
- preparing for interviews, 159–160
- quality assurance (QA), 160–161
- relaxation, 157–158
- self-monitoring of bugs, 149–150

Blue Sky, 3, 5, 12–34, 170–171
- breaking the product into pieces, 21–22
- color scheme, selection of, 27–28
- concept, 14–15
- core idea, 16–17
- design disciplines, looking at, 33–34
- fears, understanding and overcoming, 25–26
- ideas, 19–21

Blue Sky (*Continued*)
overview, 12–13
possibilities and solutions, 28–29
replay-ability, 29–30
research, 17–18
stories, 31–32
target audience, 32–33
theory *vs.* practical application of design, 22–23
thinking out of the box, 18–19
vision, 24–25
Body language, 214
Breaking things/products into pieces, 21–22
back-end levels, 21
front-end levels, 21
Breath/breathing, 180
Buddy check/system, 109, 121–122
Bugs, 117, 118–123, 181–182, 199
100% fix rate, 120–121
125% fix rate, 119–120
balancing, 122–123
buddy checks, 109, 121–122
language of, 121
listing/gathering shipped bugs, 168–169
offering assistance and fix, 148–149
self-assessment and monitoring of, 149–150
zero, 146–147
Building blocks, 84–85
Burnout, 82, 140–141

C

Camera, 55–56
three-dimensional (3-D), 55
two-dimensional (2-D), 55
Casual players, 154
Catching up with coworkers, 78–79
Celebrations, 156–157, 173–174
Change, trend followed for design, 133–134
Chaos, 107–108
handling/managing, 180–181
Character growth, 63–64
Checking/rechecking, 109–110
Class, colors selection and, 27
Colors, selection of, 27–28
class and, 27
culture and, 27
emotions/feelings and, 27
gender and, 27
location and, 27
Communication, 61–62
catching up with coworkers, 78–79
mistakes, 91
Completionist players, 154
Complexity levels, 49–50
Content
environmental, 222
items for player, 222
thought pattern/decision matrix for, 222
Content designers, 221–223
level designers as, 222
Controls, 64–65
chaos, 107–108
Copying the game. *See* Framing and putting the game on wall
Core idea, 16–17
Coworkers, catching up with, 78–79
Crazy games/competitions, 156–157
Creativity/creative time, 106–107
30-day challenge, 227–228
Crew. *See* Group
Culture, colors selection and, 27
Cut/cutting, 77–78

D

Daily routine, 152, *See also* Monotony, dealing with
Data collection, 17
Demos, 137–138
Design
documentation, 41–43
philosophy, 49–50
vs. quality assurance, 28
30-day challenge, 227–228
trend followed for change, 133–134
updating, 134–135
Design disciplines, 33–34
Designers, 210
audio, 155, 224–225
content, 221–223
interface, 219–220
level, 222, 223–224
systems, 220–221

Development cycle, 5, 13
Difficulty of game, 96–97
Disciplines, design, 33–34
Diversity, 65–66
DLC (downloadable content), 59, 195, 202–203
  planned, 195
  unplanned, 195
  vision for, 203
Document/documentation, 41–43, 135
  grand design *vs.* micro design, 42–43
Downtime, *See also* Time
  learning new tools during, 186–187
  working on ideas during, 188–189

E

Early-access offering, 138–139
Ego/ego people, 226–227
  dealing with, 226
"Elevator pitch," 16, *See also* Pitch/pitches
Emotional bias, 172
Emotions
  colors and, 27
  evoking, 48–49
  primary, 48
  secondary, 48
  tertiary, 48
End-user experience, 154–155
Enemies, in games, 82–83
Environment, 8–9
  home, 9
  travel, 9
  work, 8–9
Environmental content, 222
Evaluation method for balancing, 80
Evaluation of milestone, 76–77

F

Fashion trend. *See* Trend
Fears
  laziness and, 26
  understanding and overcoming, 25–26
Features, 21
  balancing, 92
  cut/cutting, 77–78
  fixing, 92–93, 181–182, 198–199
  interconnected, 92–93
  tuning, 94–96
Feedback, 86, 169–170
  negative, 169
  positive, 169
Final level, 164–174
  celebrations, 173–174
  concept, 166–167
  feedback, 169–170
  listing shipped bugs, 168–169
  overview, 164–165
  postmortem, 172–173
Fix/fixing
  architecting, 180
  bugs, *See* Bugs
  features, 92–93, 181–182, 198–199
  monitoring, 180
Flexibility, 131
Followers
  building/cultivating, 136–137
  vs. leaders, 213
Framing and putting the game on wall, 185–186
Fresh eyes, 151
Friends/friendship, 110–111
Front-end menu, 53, 54, *See also* Menu systems

G

Game menu, 54, *See also* Menu systems
Gender, colors selection and, 27
Genre of game, 55
Goals/goal setting, 100–101
  for details, 68–69
Goblin Encounter, 83
Golden rule of work, 225–226
Grand design document, 42–43, *See also* Micro design docs
Group, 7–8
  power hierarchy, 8

H

Hardcore players, 154
Heads-up display (HUD) menu, 54, *See also* Menu systems

Help/helping
asking for, 125–126
offering, 127–129
"Herding cats," 156–157
Hobbies, 81–82, 131
Home environment, 9
HUD. *See* Heads-up display (HUD) menu
Humility, 190

I

Idea(s), 19–21, *See also* Blue Sky
core, 16–17
Implementation levels of design, 49–50
Incentives, 86–88
Informational preparation, 4, 5
Innovation *vs.* boilerplate, 50–52
Interface design/designers, 219–220
Internet, 180
trolls/trolling, 200–201
Interviews, 159–160
Items for players, 222

K

KISS system, 213
Knowing the game, 150–151

L

Leaders, 8
vs. followers, 213
Learning new tools, 186–187
Level design, 97–98
Level designers, 223–224
as content designers, 222
Level editing tools, 223
Limitations, 19
Listening, 218
Live, 192–205
defined, 194–195
fixing existing features, 198–199
Internet trolls, 200–201
overview, 192–193
schooled by, 197–198
workflow waves, 204–205
Localization, 67–68
Locations
colors selection and, 27
players/gameplay, 154–156
Loss of self, 140

M

Maintaining balance, 80–81
Marketing, 117
approach to control trolls, 200
targeted, 117
Mental preparation, 4, 5
Menu systems, 21, 53–54, *See also* Interface design/designers
front-end menu, 53, 54
game menu, 54
heads-up display (HUD), 54
presentation of, 219
Micro design docs, 42–43, *See also* Grand design document
Milestones
evaluation of, 76–77
racing towards, 126–127
Miscellaneous skills, 208–228, *See also* Designers
avoiding/subjugating "um," 213
careful selection and usage of words, 217–219
interface design, 219–220
overview, 208–209
presentation, *See* Presentations
storytelling, *See* Storytelling
writing, 211–212
Mistakes, 90–91
communication, 91
personal, 91
professional, 91
Mobile games, 59
Models, 52–53
Monetization, 59–60
Monitoring, 195
Monotony, dealing with, 152–153

N

Narratives. *See* Stories
Negative feedback, 169

O

Offering help, 127–129
Online community, 159
Overtime. *See* Working overtime

P

Patch/patches, 181–182, 195
PC/console games, 59
PDC. *See* Player-Designer Covenant (PDC)
Personal mistakes, 91
Pitch/pitches, 16–17
Pivoting, art of, 130–131
Platform/platforms, 60–61
Player-Designer Covenant (PDC), 94
Players
 casual, 154
 completionist, 154
 hardcore, 154
 items for, 222, *See also* Content
 setting/location, 154–156
 understanding and defending needs of, 196–197
Playing the game, 153–154
 from different players perspectives, 154
 watching someone else playing game, 153
Playtest/playtesting, 85–86, 155
Positive feedback, 169
Postmortem, 172–173
Post-release, 176–190
 concept, 177–178
 framing and putting the game on wall, 185–186
 learning new tools, 186–187
 overview, 176–177
 patch/patches, 181–182
 review scores and bottom line, 184–185
 success, handling/managing, 189–190
 trolls/trolling, 180–181
 visiting products in stores, 182–183
 working on ideas during downtime, 188–189
Practical application *vs.* theory of design, 22–23
Practice and skills, 131
Praise, 169–170
Preparation, 2–9
 concept, 4–5
 crew/group, 7–8
 environment, 8–9
 informational, 4, 5
 mental, 4, 5
 overview, 2–3
 quest, 6–7
Pre-production, 36–69
 audio design, 57–58
 backstory, 46–47
 camera, 55–56
 character growth, 63–64
 communicating early, 61–62
 complexity levels, 49–50
 concept, 38–39
 controls, 64–65
 diversity, 65–66
 documentation, 41–43
 evoking emotions, *See* Emotions
 innovation *vs.* boilerplate, 50–52
 localization, 67–68
 making enemies vibrant, 82–83
 menu systems, 53–54
 models, 52–53
 monetization, 59–60
 overview, 36–37
 platform/platforms, 60–61
 prototype/prototyping, 45–46
 setting goals around details, 68–69
 time/duration, 40–41
 tools, 56–57
 writing, 44–45
Presentations
 art of, 215–216
 audiences and, 216
 menu system, 219
 preparation, 214–215
 simplicity, 214
 vocal performance for, 214
Producers, 126–127, 199
Production, 72–111
 artificial intelligence, 101–103
 building blocks, 84–85
 chaos, 107–108
 communication catch-up, 78–79

Production (*Continued*)
- concept, 74–75
- creativity/creative time, 106–107
- cut/cutting, 77–78
- difficulty, 96–97
- final feature, 103–104
- goal setting, 100–101
- incentives, 86–88
- "in" or "out" of the game, 88–89
- level design, 97–98
- maintaining balance, 80–81
- milestone evaluations, 76–77
- mistakes, 90–91
- overview, 72–73
- playtest, 85–86
- power of team, 104–105
- question/questioning oneself, 99–100
- risk *vs.* reward, 93–94
- spiderweb of features, 92–93
- stability to version, 108–110
- time being precious, 81–82
- tuning the product, 94–96
- visual storytelling, 89–90

Professional mistakes, 91
Project-planning program, 76
Prototype/prototyping, 45–46

Q

Quality assurance (QA), 28, 117, 132–133, 160–161, 180
Quest, for selected topic/mission, 6–7
Question/questioning oneself, 99–100

R

Relaxation, 157–158
- actions supporting, 158
- goals, 158

Replay-ability, 29–30
Research, 17–18
Respect, treating others with, 226
Rest, 81
Revenue, 189
Reviewers, 197, *See also* Quality assurance (QA)
Review scores, 184–185
Reward, 127, 156
"Robins," 226, *See also* "See-Mores"
Role-playing games, 83

S

Sacred art of the pivot, 130–131
Sales pitch. *See* Pitch/pitches
"See-Mores," 225–227, *See also* Ego/ego people; "Robins"
Self
- loss of, 140
- time for, 140–141

Self-doubt, 218
Shipped bugs, making list of, 168–169
Skills, 208–210, *See also* Miscellaneous skills
- combining, 208
- improvement, 186–187
- practice and, 131

Social circles, 110–111, 209–210
Social life, 204–205
Solutions, 28–29
Sound designers. *See* Audio designers
Speaking less/being silent and deadly, 217–219, *See also* Words, careful selection and usage of
Stability to version, 108–110
Stakeholders, 50
Stand-up arcade game, 30
Store/shop visit, for product, 182–183
Stories, 31–32
- backstory, 46–47
- elements of, 217
- levels of, 31

Storytelling, 216–217
- art of, 216
- defined, 216
- elements of, 217
- visual, 89–90

Success, handling/managing, 189–190
Systems designers, 220–221

T

Target audience, 32–33
Targeted marketing, 117
Team power, 104–105, *See also* Group

Technical issues, 197–198
Test/testing, 123–124
  A/B testing, 201–202
  engineering group and, 201
  hypothesis, 201–202
  playtesting, 85–86
Theory *vs.* practical application of design, 22–23
Thinking out of the box, 18–19
Three-dimensional (3-D) camera, 55
Three-dimensional design, 219
Time, 40–41
  for creativity/being creative, 106–107
  importance, 81–82
  scheduling, 118
  you moment, 140–141
Time management, 187
Tools, 56–57
  learning, 186–187
Trend, 133–134
Trolls/trolling, 180–181
  converted into heroes, 200–201
  marketing approach to control, 200
Trophy, 156
Tuning the product, 94–96
  review sessions, 95
Two-dimensional (2-D) camera, 55
Two-dimensional design, 219

U

"Um," 212–213
  avoiding/subjugating, 213
  described, 212
Updating design, 134–135
Users. *See* Players

V

Verbal cues, 214
Version stability, 108–110
Vision, 24–25
Visiting products in stores, 182–183
Visual storytelling, 89–90

W

Well-received game, 222
Win/winning. *See* Success, handling/managing
Words, careful selection and usage of, 217–219
Work
  environment, 8–9
  golden rule of, 225–226
Workflow, live period, 204–205
Working overtime, 82, 126–127
  dealing with the madness of, 129–130
Writing, 44–45
  practicing, 211–212

Y

You time/moment, 140–141, *See also* Self

Z

Zero bugs, 146–147